To the Instructor

Thank you for your interest in the Townsend Press vocabulary series—the most widely-used vocabulary books on the college market today. Our goal in this series has been to produce nothing less than excellent books at nothing more than reasonable prices.

About the Book

Notice that the introduction to students (page 1) immediately makes clear to them just why vocabulary study is important. Students are motivated to learn by the four compelling kinds of evidence for word study. The back cover as well convinces students that "a solid vocabulary is a source of power."

You may want to look then at the preface, starting on page vii, which describes in detail the nine distinctive features of the book.

You'll see that a second color is used in the text to make the material as inviting as possible. You'll note, too, that while each chapter takes up only four pages, those pages contain a great deal of hands-on practice to help ensure that students master each word. And you'll find that the practice materials themselves are far more carefully done, and more appealing, than the run-of-the-mill items you typically find in a skills text. The quality and interest level of the content will help students truly learn the words, without either boring them or insulting their intelligence.

Supplements to the Book

Adding to the value of *Advancing Vocabulary Skills, Short Version*, which has a net price of only $8.40, is the quality of the supplements:

- An *Instructor's Edition*, which you hold in your hand. The Instructor's Edition is identical to the student text except that it includes (in *color*) the answers to all of the practices and tests.

- A combined *Instructor's Manual and Test Bank*, free with adoptions of 20 or more copies. This booklet contains a general vocabulary placement test as well as a pretest and a posttest for the book and for each of the four units in the text. It also includes teaching guidelines, suggested syllabi, an answer key, and an additional mastery test for each chapter as well as an additional mastery test for each unit.

- *Computer software* in Windows or Macintosh format, which provides a general placement test and two additional tests for each vocabulary chapter in the book. Free with adoptions of 20 or more copies, the software tests contain a number of user- and instructor-friendly features, including actual, audible pronunciations of the words; brief explanations of answers; a sound option; mouse support; frequent mention of the user's first name; a running score at the bottom of the screen; and a record-keeping file.

Adopters of the book can obtain these supplements by calling our toll-free number, 1-800-772-6410, or by writing, e-mailing, or faxing Townsend Press at the numbers on page iv.

(Continues on next page)

New Features of the Book

Among the changes in this Third Edition of *Advancing Vocabulary Skills, Short Version,* are the following:

- Test 4 in each set of unit tests now consists of twenty word analogies, and a section on analogies has been added to the introduction.

- The remaining unit tests have been extensively revised, and a new multiple-choice section, involving using the words in realistic situations, has been added to Test 1 in each set.

- A new section, "Topics for Discussion and Writing," provides six high-interest items for each of the vocabulary chapters. Each item uses one or more of the words in the chapter in a brief scenario suitable for class or small-group discussion, writing, or both.

- Finally, a number of practice items throughout the book have been revised or updated to ensure that each item works as clearly and effectively with students as possible.

A Comprehensive Vocabulary Program

There are nine books in the Townsend Press vocabulary series:

- *Vocabulary Basics* (reading level 4–6)
- *Groundwork for a Better Vocabulary* (reading level 5–8)
- *Building Vocabulary Skills* (reading level 7–9)
- *Building Vocabulary Skills, Short Version* (reading level 7–9)
- *Improving Vocabulary Skills* (reading level 9–11)
- *Improving Vocabulary Skills, Short Version* (reading level 9–11)
- *Advancing Vocabulary Skills* (reading level 11–13)
- *Advancing Vocabulary Skills, Short Version* (reading level 11–13)
- *Advanced Word Power* (reading level 12–14)

Note that the short versions of the three books are limited to 200 words, as opposed to the 260 words and 40 word parts in each of the long versions. For some students and classes, the short versions of the book will provide an easier, more manageable approach to vocabulary development.

ADVANCING VOCABULARY SKILLS

SHORT VERSION / Third Edition

SHERRIE L. NIST
UNIVERSITY OF GEORGIA

CAROLE MOHR

TOWNSEND PRESS

Books in the Townsend Press Vocabulary Series:

Vocabulary Basics
Groundwork for a Better Vocabulary
Building Vocabulary Skills
Building Vocabulary Skills, Short Version
Improving Vocabulary Skills
Improving Vocabulary Skills, Short Version
Advancing Vocabulary Skills
Advancing Vocabulary Skills, Short Version
Advanced Word Power

Books in the Townsend Press Reading Series:

Groundwork for College Reading
Ten Steps to Building College Reading Skills
Ten Steps to Improving College Reading Skills
Ten Steps to Advancing College Reading Skills

Other Reading and Writing Books:

Everyday Heroes
A Basic Reader for College Writers
The Townsend Thematic Reader
Voices and Values: A Reader for Writers
English at Hand

Supplements Available for Most Books:

Instructor's Edition
Instructor's Manual and Test Bank
Computer Software (Windows or Macintosh)

Copyright © 2002 by Townsend Press, Inc.
Printed in the United States of America
ISBN 0-944210-17-1
9 8 7 6 5 4 3 2 1

Send book orders and requests for desk copies or supplements to:
Townsend Press Book Center
1038 Industrial Drive
West Berlin, New Jersey 08091

For even faster service, contact us in any of the following ways:
By telephone: 1-800-772-6410
By fax: 1-800-225-8894
By e-mail: TownsendCS@aol.com
Through our website: www.townsendpress.com

Contents

Note: For ease of reference, the title of the selection that closes each chapter is included.

UNIT FOUR

APPENDIXES

Preface

The problem is all too familiar: *students just don't know enough words.* Reading, writing, and content teachers agree that many students' vocabularies are inadequate for the demands of courses. Weak vocabularies limit students' understanding of what they read and the clarity and depth of what they write.

The purpose of the Townsend Press vocabulary series is to provide a solid, workable answer to the vocabulary problem. The short version of the series consists of three books, each of which teaches 200 important words. Within each book are twenty chapters, with ten words in each chapter. Here are the distinctive features of *Advancing Vocabulary Skills, Short Version, Third Edition:*

1 **An intensive words-in-context approach.** Studies show that students learn words best by reading them repeatedly in different contexts, not through rote memorization. The book gives students an intensive in-context experience by presenting each word in six different contexts. Each chapter takes students through a productive sequence of steps:

- Students infer the meaning of each word by considering two sentences in which it appears and then choosing from multiple-choice options.
- On the basis of their inferences, students identify each word's meaning in a matching test. They are then in a solid position to deepen their knowledge of a word.
- Finally, they strengthen their understanding of a word by applying it three times: in two sentence practices and in a selection practice.

Each encounter with a word brings it closer to becoming part of the student's permanent word bank.

2 **Abundant practice.** Along with extensive practice in each chapter, there are a crossword puzzle and a set of unit tests at the end of every five-chapter unit. The puzzle and tests reinforce students' knowledge of the words in each chapter. In addition, most chapters reuse several words from earlier chapters (such repeated words are marked with small circles), allowing for more reinforcement. Last, there are supplementary tests in the *Test Bank* and the computer software that accompany the book. All this practice means that students learn in the surest possible way: by working closely and repeatedly with each word.

3 **Controlled feedback.** The opening activity in each chapter gives students three multiple-choice options to help them decide on the meaning of a given word. The multiple-choice options also help students to complete the matching test that is the second activity of each chapter. A limited answer key at the back of the book then provides answers for the third activity in the chapter. All these features enable students to take an active role in their own learning.

4 **Focus on essential words.** A good deal of time and research went into selecting the 200 words featured in the book. Word frequency lists were consulted, along with lists in a wide range of vocabulary books. In addition, the authors and editors each prepared their own lists. A computer was used to help in the consolidation of the many word lists. A long process of group discussion then led to final decisions about the words that would be most helpful for students on a basic reading level.

5 **Appealing content.** Dull practice materials work against learning. On the other hand, meaningful, lively, and at times even funny sentences and selections can spark students' attention and thus enhance their grasp of the material. For this reason, a great deal of effort was put into creating sentences and selections with both widespread appeal and solid context support. We have tried throughout to make the practice materials truly enjoyable for teachers and students alike. Look, for example, at the selection on page 11 that closes the first chapter of this book.

6 **Clear format.** The book has been designed so that its very format contributes to the learning process. Each chapter consists of two two-page spreads. In the first two-page spread (the first such spread is on pages 8–9), students can easily refer to all ten words in context while working on the matching test, which provides a clear meaning for each word. In the second two-page spread, students can refer to a box that shows all ten words while they work through the fill-in activities on these pages.

7 **Supplementary materials.**

a A convenient *Instructor's Edition* is available at no charge to instructors using the book. It is identical to the student book except that it contains answers to all of the activities and tests.

b A combined *Instructor's Manual and Test Bank* is also offered at no charge to instructors who have adopted the book. This booklet contains a general vocabulary placement test as well as a pretest and a posttest for the book and for each of the four units in the text. It also includes teaching guidelines, suggested syllabi, an answer key, and an additional mastery test for each chapter as well as an additional mastery test for each unit.

c *Interactive computer software* also accompanies the book. Free to adopters of 20 or more copies, this software—in both Windows and Macintosh format—provides two additional tests for each vocabulary chapter in the book. The tests include a number of user- and instructor-friendly features: brief explanations of answers (thus the software teaches as well as tests), a sound option, mouse support, icons, color, dialog balloons, frequent mention of the user's first name, a running score at the bottom of the screen, a record-keeping file, and actual, audible pronunciations of each word. Students can access their scores at any time; instructors can access student scores by selecting Administrator mode and entering the appropriate password.

Probably in no other area of reading instruction is the computer more useful than in reinforcing vocabulary. The Townsend Press vocabulary software takes full advantage of the computer's unique capabilities and motivational appeal. Here's how the program works:

• Students are tested on the ten words in a chapter, with each word in a sentence context different from any in the book itself.

• After students answer each question, they receive immediate feedback: The computer indicates if a student is right or wrong and why, frequently using the student's first name and providing a running score.

• When the test is over, the computer supplies a test score and—this especially is what is unique about this program—a chance to take the test a second time. Students then receive a separate score for the retest. The value of this approach is that the computer gives students immediate added practice in words they need to review.

• In addition, the computer offers a second, more challenging "Definitions" test in which students must identify the meanings of the chapter words without benefit of context. This test is a final check that students have really learned the words. And, again, there is the option of a retest.

By the end of this program, students' knowledge of each word in the chapter will have been carefully reinforced. And this reinforcement will be the more effective for having occurred in an electronic medium that especially engages today's students.

To obtain a copy of any of the above materials, instructors who have adopted the book may write to the Reading Editor, Townsend Press, 1038 Industrial Drive, West Berlin, NJ 08091. Alternatively, instructors may call our toll-free number: 1-800-772-6410; send a fax toll-free to 1-800-225-8894, or e-mail our Customer Service department at <townsendcs@aol.com>.

8 **Realistic pricing.** As with the previous editions, the goal has been to offer the highest possible quality at the best possible price. While *Advancing Vocabulary Skills, Short Version* is comprehensive enough to serve as a primary text, its modest price also makes it an inexpensive supplement.

9 **One in a sequence of books.** The most fundamental book in the Townsend Press vocabulary series is *Vocabulary Basics*. It is followed by *Groundwork for a Better Vocabulary* (a slightly more advanced basic text) and then by the three main books in the series: *Building Vocabulary Skills* (also a basic text), *Improving Vocabulary Skills* (an intermediate text), and *Advancing Vocabulary Skills* (a more advanced text). The most advanced book in the Townsend Press vocabulary series is *Advanced Word Power*. There are also short versions of the *Building, Improving*, and *Advancing* books, one of which is this book, *Advancing Vocabulary Skills, Short Version, Third Edition*. Suggested grade levels for the books are included in the *Instructor's Manual*. Together, the books can help create a vocabulary foundation that will make any student a better reader, writer, and thinker.

NOTES ON THE THIRD EDITION

A number of changes have been made in the third edition of *Advancing Vocabulary Skills, Short Version:*

- Material on how to solve word analogies has been added to the introduction, and a new unit test consisting of twenty word analogies has been prepared for each unit in the book. These tests provide practice in a format widely used in standardized tests.

- The remaining unit tests have been extensively revised, and a new multiple-choice section, using the words in realistic situations, has been added to Test 1 throughout.

- A new section, "Topics for Discussion and Writing," provides six high-interest items for each of the vocabulary chapters. Each item uses one or more of the vocabulary words in the chapter in a brief scenario suitable for class or small-group discussion, writing, or both.

- Finally, a number of practice items throughout the book have been revised or updated to ensure that each item works as clearly and effectively with students as possible.

ACKNOWLEDGMENTS

We are grateful for the enthusiastic comments provided by users of the Townsend Press vocabulary books over the life of the first and second editions. We appreciate as well the additional material provided by Beth Johnson, Susan Gamer, and Eleanor Tauber; the editing work of Eliza Comodromos; the proofreading work of Barbara Solot; and, especially, the organizational, design, and editing skills of the indefatigable Janet M. Goldstein.

Sherrie L. Nist   *Carole Mohr*

Introduction

WHY VOCABULARY DEVELOPMENT COUNTS

You have probably often heard it said, "Building vocabulary is important." Maybe you've politely nodded in agreement and then forgotten the matter. But it would be fair for you to ask, "*Why* is vocabulary development important? Provide some evidence." Here are four compelling kinds of evidence.

1 Common sense tells you what many research studies have shown as well: vocabulary is a basic part of reading comprehension. Simply put, if you don't know enough words, you are going to have trouble understanding what you read. An occasional word may not stop you, but if there are too many words you don't know, comprehension will suffer. The content of textbooks is often challenge enough; you don't want to work as well on understanding the words that express that content.

2 Vocabulary is a major part of almost every standardized test, including reading achievement tests, college entrance exams, and armed forces and vocational placement tests. Test developers know that vocabulary is a key measure of both one's learning and one's ability to learn. It is for this reason that they include a separate vocabulary section as well as a reading comprehension section. The more words you know, then, the better you are likely to do on such important tests.

3 Studies have indicated that students with strong vocabularies are more successful in school. And one widely known study found that a good vocabulary, more than any other factor, was common to people enjoying successful careers in life. Words are in fact the tools not just of better reading, but of better writing, speaking, listening, and thinking as well. The more words you have at your command, the more effective your communication can be, and the more influence you can have on the people around you.

4 In today's world, a good vocabulary counts more than ever. Far fewer people work on farms or in factories. Far more are in jobs that provide services or process information. More than ever, words are the tools of our trade: words we use in reading, writing, listening, and speaking. Furthermore, experts say that workers of tomorrow will be called on to change jobs and learn new skills at an ever-increasing pace. The keys to survival and success will be the abilities to communicate skillfully and learn quickly. A solid vocabulary is essential for both of these skills.

Clearly, the evidence is overwhelming that building vocabulary is crucial. The question then becomes, "What is the best way of going about it?"

WORDS IN CONTEXT: THE KEY TO VOCABULARY DEVELOPMENT

Memorizing lists of words is a traditional method of vocabulary development. However, a person is likely to forget such memorized lists quickly. Studies show that to master a word, you must see and use it in various contexts. By working actively and repeatedly with a word, you greatly increase the chance of really learning it.

The following activity will make clear how this book is organized and how it uses a words-in-context approach. Answer the questions or fill in the missing words in the spaces provided.

Inside Front Cover and Contents

Turn to the inside front cover.

- The inside front cover provides a _____*pronunciation guide*_____ that will help you pronounce all the vocabulary words in the book.

Now turn to the table of contents on pages v–vi.

- How many chapters are in the book? ___*20*___

- Four sections follow the last chapter. The first of these sections provides a limited answer key, the second gives helpful information on using _____*the dictionary*_____, the third contains ___*topics for*___ _____*discussion and writing*_____, and the fourth is an index of the 200 words in the book.

Vocabulary Chapters

Turn to Chapter 1 on pages 8–11. This chapter, like all the others, consists of five parts:

- The ***first part*** of the chapter, on pages 8–9, is titled _____*Ten Words in Context*_____.

  The left-hand column lists the ten words. Under each **boldfaced** word is its _____*pronunciation*_____ (in parentheses). For example, the pronunciation of *detriment* is _____*dĕ′trə-mənt*_____. For a guide to pronunciation, see the inside front cover as well as "Dictionary Use" on page 131.

  Below the pronunciation guide for each word is its part of speech. The part of speech shown for *detriment* is _____*noun*_____. The vocabulary words in this book are mostly nouns, adjectives, and verbs. **Nouns** are words used to name something—a person, place, thing, or idea. Familiar nouns include *boyfriend, city, hat,* and *truth.* **Adjectives** are words that describe nouns, as in the following word pairs: *former* boyfriend, *large* city, *red* hat, *whole* truth. All of the **verbs** in this book express an action of some sort. They tell what someone or something is doing. Common verbs include *sing, separate, support,* and *imagine.*

  To the right of each word are two sentences that will help you understand its meaning. In each sentence, the **context**—the words surrounding the boldfaced word—provides clues you can use to figure out the definition. There are four common types of context clues—examples, synonyms, antonyms, and the general sense of the sentence. Each is briefly described below.

  1 Examples

  A sentence may include examples that reveal what an unfamiliar word means. For instance, take a look at the following sentence from Chapter 1 for the word *scrupulous*:

  The judge was **scrupulous** about never accepting a bribe or allowing a personal threat to influence his decisions.

  The sentence provides two examples of what makes the judge scrupulous. The first is that he never accepted a bribe. The second is that the judge did not allow personal threats to influence his decisions. What do these two examples have in common? The answer to that question will tell you what *scrupulous* means. Look at the answer choices below, and in the answer space provided, write the letter of the one you feel is correct.

    _a_ *Scrupulous* means   a. ethical.   b. economical.   c. unjust.

Both of the examples given in the sentences about the judge tell us that he is honest, or *ethical*. So if you wrote *a*, you chose the correct answer.

2 Synonyms

Synonyms are words that mean the same or almost the same as another word. For example, the words *joyful, happy,* and *delighted* are synonyms—they all mean about the same thing. Synonyms serve as context clues by providing the meaning of an unknown word that is nearby. The sentence below from Chapter 2 provides a synonym clue for *collaborate.*

> When Sarah and I were asked to **collaborate** on an article for the school newspaper, we found it difficult to work together.

Instead of using *collaborate* twice, the author used a synonym in the second part of the sentence. Find that synonym, and then choose the letter of the correct answer from the choices below.

    _c_ *Collaborate* means   a. to compete.   b. to stop work.   c. to team up.

The author uses two terms to express what Sarah and the speaker had to do: *collaborate* and *work together*. Therefore, *collaborate* must be another way of saying *work together*. (The author could have written, "Sarah and I were asked to *work together*.") Since *work together* can also mean *team up*, the correct answer is *c*.

3 Antonyms

Antonyms are words with opposite meanings. For example, *help* and *harm* are antonyms, as are *work* and *rest*. Antonyms serve as context clues by providing the opposite meaning of an unknown word. For instance, the sentence below from Chapter 1 provides an antonym clue for the word *gregarious.*

> My **gregarious** brother loves parties, but my shy sister prefers to be alone.

The author is contrasting the brother's and sister's different personalities, so we can assume that *gregarious* and *shy* have opposite, or contrasting, meanings. Using that contrast as a clue, write the letter of the answer that you think best defines *gregarious.*

    _b_ *Gregarious* means   a. attractive.   b. outgoing.   c. humorous.

The correct answer is *b*. Because *gregarious* is the opposite of *shy*, it must mean "outgoing."

4 General Sense of the Sentence

Even when there is no example, synonym, or antonym clue in a sentence, you can still deduce the meaning of an unfamiliar word. For example, look at the sentence from Chapter 1 for the word *detriment.*

> Smoking is a **detriment** to your health. It's estimated that each cigarette you smoke will shorten your life by one and a half minutes.

After studying the context carefully, you should be able to figure out the connection between smoking and health. That will be the meaning of *detriment*. Write the letter of your choice.

    _c_ *Detriment* means   a. an aid.   b. a discovery.   c. a disadvantage.

Since the sentence says that each cigarette will shorten the smoker's life by one and a half minutes, it is logical to conclude that smoking has a bad effect on health. Thus answer *c* is correct.

By looking closely at the pair of sentences provided for each word, as well as the answer choices, you should be able to decide on the meaning of a word. As you figure out each meaning, you are working actively with the word. You are creating the groundwork you need to understand and to remember the word. *Getting involved with the word and developing a feel for it, based upon its use in context, is the key to word mastery.*

It is with good reason, then, that the directions at the top of page 8 tell you to use the context to figure out each word's _____*meaning*_____. Doing so deepens your sense of the word and prepares you for the next activity.

- The *second part* of the chapter, on page 9, is titled _____*Matching Words with Definitions*_____.

According to research, it is not enough to see a word in context. At a certain point, it is helpful as well to see the meaning of a word. The matching test provides that meaning, but it also makes you look for and think about that meaning. In other words, it continues the active learning that is your surest route to learning and remembering a word.

Note the caution that follows the test. Do not proceed any further until you are sure that you know the correct meaning of each word as used in context.

Keep in mind that a word may have more than one meaning. In fact, some words have quite a few meanings. (If you doubt it, try looking up in a dictionary, for example, the word *make* or *draw*.) In this book, you will focus on one common meaning for each vocabulary word. However, many of the words have additional meanings. For example, in Chapter 1, you will learn that *discretion* means "good judgment," as in the sentence "Ali wasn't using much discretion when he passed a police car at eighty miles an hour." If you then look up *discretion* in the dictionary, you will discover that it has another meaning—"freedom to act on one's own," as in "All the arrangements for the event were left to our discretion." After you learn one common meaning of a word, you will find yourself gradually learning its other meanings in the course of your school and personal reading.

- The *third part* of the chapter, on page 10, is titled _____*Sentence Check 1*_____.

Here are ten sentences that give you an opportunity to apply your understanding of the ten words. After inserting the words, check your answers in the limited key at the back of the book. Be sure to use the answer key as a learning tool only. Doing so will help you to master the words and to prepare for the last two activities and the unit tests, for which answers are not provided.

- The *fourth and fifth parts* of the chapter, on pages 10–11, are titled _____*Sentence Check 2*_____ and _____*Final Check*_____.

Each practice tests you on all ten words, giving you two more chances to deepen your mastery. In the fifth part, you have the context of an entire passage in which you can practice applying the words.

At the bottom of the last page of this chapter is a box where you can enter your score for the final two checks. These scores should also be entered into the vocabulary performance chart located on the inside back page of the book. To get your score, take 10% off for each item wrong. For example, 0 wrong = 100%. 1 wrong = 90%, 2 wrong = 80%, 3 wrong = 70%, 4 wrong = 60%, and so on.

You now know, in a nutshell, how to proceed with the words in each chapter. Make sure that you do each page very carefully. *Remember that as you work through the activities, you are learning the words.*

How many times in all will you use each word? If you look, you'll see that each chapter gives you the opportunity to work with each word six times. Each "impression" adds to the likelihood that the word will become part of your active vocabulary. You will have further opportunities to use the word in the crossword puzzle and unit tests that end each unit and on the computer disks that are available with the book.

In addition, many of the words are repeated in context in later chapters of the book. Such repeated words are marked with small circles. For example, which words from Chapter 1 are repeated in the Final Check on page 15 of Chapter 2?

_____*optimum*_____   _____*detriment*_____

Analogies

This book also offers practice in word analogies, yet another way to deepen your understanding of words. An **analogy** is a similarity between two things that are otherwise different. Doing an analogy question is a two-step process. First you have to figure out the relationship in a pair of words. Those words are written like this:

LEAF : TREE

What is the relationship between the two words above? The answer can be stated like this: A leaf is a part of a tree.

Next, you must look for a similar relationship in a second pair of words. Here is how a complete analogy question looks:

LEAF : TREE ::

a. pond : river   b. foot : shoe
c. page : book   d. beach : sky

And here is how the question can be read:

_c_ LEAF is to TREE as

a. *pond* is to *river.*   b. *foot* is to *shoe.*
c. *page* is to *book.*   d. *beach* is to *sky.*

To answer the question, you have to decide which of the four choices has a relationship similar to the first one. Check your answer by seeing if it fits in the same wording as you used to show the relationship between *leaf* and *tree:* A ___ is part of a ___. Which answer do you choose?

The correct answer is *c.* Just as a *leaf* is part of a *tree,* a *page* is part of a *book.* On the other hand, a *pond* is not part of a *river,* nor is a *foot* part of a *shoe,* nor is a *beach* part of the *sky.*

We can state the complete analogy this way: *Leaf* is to *tree* as *page* is to *book.*

Here's another analogy question to try. Begin by figuring out the relationship between the first two words.

_d_ COWARD : HERO ::

a. soldier : military   b. infant : baby
c. actor : famous   d. boss : worker

Coward and *hero* are opposite types of people. So you need to look at the other four pairs to see which has a similar relationship. When you think you have found the answer, check to see that the two words you chose can be compared in the same way as *coward* and *hero:* ___ and ___ are opposite types of people.

In this case, the correct answer is *d*; *boss* and *worker* are opposite kinds of people. (In other words, *coward* is to *hero* as *boss* is to *worker.*)

By now you can see that there are basically two steps to doing analogy items:

1) Find out the relationship of the first two words.
2) Find the answer that expresses the same type of relationship as the first two words have.

Now try one more analogy question on your own. Write the letter of the answer you choose in the space provided.

_a_ SWING : BAT ::

a. drive : car   b. run : broom
c. catch : bat   d. fly : butterfly

If you chose answer *a,* you were right. *Swing* is what we do with a *bat,* and *drive* is what we do with a *car.*

A FINAL THOUGHT

The facts are in. A strong vocabulary is a source of power. Words can make you a better reader, writer, speaker, thinker, and learner. They can dramatically increase your chances of success in school and in your job.

But words will not come automatically. They must be learned in a program of regular study. If you commit yourself to learning words, and you work actively and honestly with the chapters in this book, you will not only enrich your vocabulary—you will enrich your life as well.

Unit One

CHAPTER

1

detriment	optimum
dexterous	ostentatious
discretion	scrupulous
facetious	sensory
gregarious	vicarious

Ten Words in Context

In the space provided, write the letter of the meaning closest to that of each **boldfaced** word. Use the context of the sentences to help you figure out each word's meaning.

1 detriment
(dĕ′trə-mənt)
-noun

- Loni's purple hair may be a **detriment** when she goes for a job interview.
- Smoking is a **detriment** to your health. It's estimated that each cigarette you smoke will shorten your life by one and a half minutes.

_c_ *Detriment* means   a. an aid.   b. a discovery.   c. a disadvantage.

2 dexterous
(dĕks′tər-əs)
-adjective

- The juggler was so **dexterous** that he managed to keep five balls in motion at once.
- Although he has arthritis in his hands, Phil is very **dexterous**. For example, he builds detailed model airplanes.

_a_ *Dexterous* means   a. skilled.   b. educated.   c. awkward.

3 discretion
(dĭ-skrĕsh′ən)
-noun

- Ali wasn't using much **discretion** when he passed a police car at eighty miles an hour.
- Small children haven't yet developed **discretion**. They ask embarrassing questions like "When will you be dead, Grandpa?"

_b_ *Discretion* means   a. skill.   b. good sense.   c. courage.

4 facetious
(fə-sē′shəs)
-adjective

- Dr. Segura has a **facetious** sign on his office door: "I'd like to help you out. Which way did you come in?"
- My boss always says, "You don't have to be crazy to work here, but it helps." I hope she's just being **facetious**.

_c_ *Facetious* means   a. serious.   b. dishonest.   c. funny.

5 gregarious
(grĭ-gâr′ē-əs)
-adjective

- Melissa is so **gregarious** that she wants to be with other people even when she's studying.
- My **gregarious** brother loves parties, but my shy sister prefers to be alone.

_b_ *Gregarious* means   a. attractive.   b. outgoing.   c. humorous.

6 optimum
(ŏp′tə-məm)
-adjective

- The road was so icy that the **optimum** driving speed was only about ten miles an hour.
- For the weary traveler, **optimum** hotel accommodations include a quiet room, a comfortable bed, and efficient room service.

_a_ *Optimum* means   a. ideal.   b. hopeful.   c. questionable.

7 ostentatious
(ŏs′tən-tā′shəs)
-*adjective*

- My show-off aunt has some **ostentatious** jewelry, such as a gold bracelet that's so heavy she can hardly lift her arm.
- The lobby of that hotel is **ostentatious**, with fancy furniture, thick rugs, and tall flower arrangements. The guest rooms upstairs, however, are extremely plain.

_b_ *Ostentatious* means   a. humble.   b. showy.   c. clean.

8 scrupulous
(skrōō′pyə-ləs)
-*adjective*

- The judge was **scrupulous** about never accepting a bribe or allowing a personal threat to influence his decisions.
- The senator promised to run a **scrupulous** campaign, but her ads were filled with lies about her opponent's personal life.

_a_ *Scrupulous* means   a. ethical.   b. economical.   c. unjust.

9 sensory
(sĕn′sə-rē)
-*adjective*

- Since our **sensory** experiences are interrelated, what we taste is greatly influenced by what we smell.
- A person in a flotation tank has almost no **sensory** stimulation. The tank is dark and soundproof, and the person floats in water at body temperature, unable to see or hear and scarcely able to feel anything.

_a_ *Sensory* means   a. of the senses.   b. social.   c. intellectual.

10 vicarious
(vī-kâr′ē-əs)
-*adjective*

- I don't like to take risks myself, but I love the **vicarious** thrill of watching death-defying adventures in a movie.
- If you can't afford to travel, reading guidebooks can give you a **vicarious** experience of traveling in foreign countries.

_b_ *Vicarious* means   a. thorough.   b. indirect.   c. skillful.

Matching Words with Definitions

Following are definitions of the ten words. Clearly write or print each word next to its definition. The sentences above and on the previous page will help you decide on the meaning of each word.

1.   *facetious*   Humorous; playfully joking

2.   *ostentatious*   Meant to impress others; flashy

3.   *optimum*   Best possible; most favorable; most desirable

4.   *detriment*   Something that causes damage, harm, or loss

5.   *vicarious*   Experienced through the imagination; not experienced directly

6.   *dexterous*   Skillful in using the hands or body

7.   *scrupulous*   Careful about moral standards; conscientious

8.   *gregarious*   Sociable; enjoying and seeking the company of others

9.   *discretion*   Good judgment or tact in actions or speaking

10.   *sensory*   Having to do with seeing, hearing, feeling, tasting, or smelling

CAUTION: Do not go any further until you are sure the above answers are correct. Then you can use the definitions to help you in the following practices. Your goal is eventually to know the words well enough so that you don't need to check the definitions at all.

➤ *Sentence Check 1*

Using the answer line provided, complete each item below with the correct word from the box. Use each word once.

a. **detriment**	b. **dexterous**	c. **discretion**	d. **facetious**	e. **gregarious**
f. **optimum**	g. **ostentatious**	h. **scrupulous**	i. **sensory**	j. **vicarious**

discretion   1. Any employee who wants to use ___ would simply ignore a piece of spinach on the boss's front tooth.

detriment   2. A weak voice is a serious ___ to a stage actor's or actress's career.

dexterous   3. Playing with blocks and puzzles makes children more ___ with their hands.

gregarious   4. My roommate used to be ___, but since he was mugged, he's begun to avoid people.

scrupulous   5. Lonnie is so ___ about filling out his tax return that he even reported the $12.50 he was paid for jury duty.

ostentatious   6. Jasmine wants to practice her vocabulary skills, so she's not just being ___ when she uses long words.

vicarious   7. Do you think a spectator sport gives the fans ___ triumphs and defeats, or real ones?

optimum   8. The ___ order in which to answer test questions is from easiest to most difficult, so that you can write the answers you know before time runs out.

sensory   9. Wandering through the bee-filled fields of red and yellow flowers was an amazing ___ experience, one that appealed to the eyes, ears, and nose.

facetious   10. The performer Oscar Levant had a tendency to cause disasters. He once made the ___ comment, "In my hands, Jell-O is a deadly weapon."

NOTE: Now check your answers to these questions by turning to page 129. Going over the answers carefully will help you prepare for the next two practices, for which answers are not given.

➤ *Sentence Check 2*

Using the answer lines provided, complete each item below with **two** words from the box. Use each word once.

discretion
scrupulous   1–2. "You have to use ___ in choosing your friends," my father said. "If your associates are dishonest, people will think that you yourself may not be ___."

facetious
dexterous   3–4. Tyra is being ___ when she says she's as ___ a dancer as a ballerina. That's her way of making fun of her own clumsiness.

optimum
detriment   5–6. When you take vitamins, be sure to take only the recommended dose. Anything more than this ___ amount can be a dangerous ___ to your health.

_____ *gregarious* _____   7–8. My neighbors give a lot of parties, but not because they're ___. They
_____ *ostentatious* _____   just want to impress the guests with their ___ home and furnishings.

_____ *sensory* _____   9–10. Our cousin in Nigeria writes great letters, filled with ___ details that
_____ *vicarious* _____   give us a(n) ___ acquaintance with the sights and sounds of an African
                                       village.

➤ *Final Check:* Apartment Problems

Here is a final opportunity for you to strengthen your knowledge of the ten words. First read the following selection carefully. Then fill in each blank with a word from the box at the top of the previous page. (Context clues will help you figure out which word goes in which blank.) Use each word once.

Although I'm ordinarily a(n) (1)_____ *gregarious* _____ person, I'm tempted to move into a cave, far from other people—and landlords. Okay, I admit that I didn't use enough (2)_____ *discretion* _____ in choosing apartments to rent. But does every one of them have to be a (3)_____ *detriment* _____ to my health, mental stability, and checkbook?

When I moved into my first apartment, I discovered that the previous tenant had already subleased the place to a very large family—of cockroaches. Although I kept trying, I was never (4)_____ *dexterous* _____ enough to swat any of them; they were able to dodge all my blows. In time, they became so bold that they paraded across the kitchen floor in the daytime in a(n) (5)_____ *ostentatious* _____ manner meant to impress upon me how useless it was to try to stop them. As soon as I could, I moved out.

My second apartment was a(n) (6)_____ *sensory* _____ nightmare—the filth was hard on the eyes and the nose. The place even assaulted the ears, as the walls were as thin as cardboard. My neighbors played music until all hours. Since I was too poor to buy a stereo, I became a dedicated listener. I even attended some of the neighbors' parties, in a(n) (7)_____ *vicarious* _____ way—with my ear to the wall. When my landlord found out, he tried to charge me seven dollars a day for entertainment, and he wasn't being (8)_____ *facetious* _____ —he meant it. I moved again, hoping to find a decent, (9)_____ *scrupulous* _____ landlord.

I rented my last apartment because it was supposedly located in an area of (10)_____ *optimum* _____ safety, considering the rent I can afford. A week after I moved in, I came home to find the locks broken and my belongings all over the floor. On the dresser was an angry note: "What gives you the right to live in such a nice neighborhood and not have anything worth stealing?"

Maybe I should have stayed with the cockroaches. At least they were honest.

Scores Sentence Check 2 _____%	Final Check _____%

Enter your scores above and in the vocabulary performance chart on the inside back cover of the book.

collaborate	rudimentary
despondent	scoff
instigate	squelch
resilient	venerate
retrospect	zealot

Ten Words in Context

In the space provided, write the letter of the meaning closest to that of each **boldfaced** word. Use the context of the sentences to help you figure out each word's meaning.

1 collaborate
(kə-lăb′ə-rāt)
-*verb*

- When Sarah and I were asked to **collaborate** on an article for the school newspaper, we found it difficult to work together.
- Several writers and editors have **collaborated** in preparing this vocabulary text, sharing their knowledge and skills.

c *Collaborate* means
   a. to compete.
   b. to stop work.
   c. to team up.

2 despondent
(dĭ-spŏn′dənt)
-*adjective*

- Devon becomes **despondent** too easily. If he gets even one bad grade, he loses all hope of succeeding in school.
- For months after his wife died, Mr. Craig was **despondent**. He even considered suicide.

b *Despondent* means
   a. ill.
   b. depressed.
   c. angry.

3 instigate
(ĭn′stə-gāt′)
-*verb*

- The rock group's violent performance **instigated** a riot in the audience.
- An English captain named Robert Jenkins **instigated** a war in 1738 by displaying his pickled ear, which he said had been cut off by a Spanish patrol. The horrified British declared war on Spain—the "War of Jenkins' Ear."

c *Instigate* means
   a. to prevent.
   b. to predict.
   c. to cause.

4 resilient
(rĭ-zĭl′yənt)
-*adjective*

- Children can be amazingly **resilient**. Having faced sad and frightening experiences, they often bounce back to their normal cheerful selves.
- Plant life is **resilient**. For example, a few weeks after the Mount St. Helens volcano erupted in Washington in 1980, flowers were growing in the ashes.

c *Resilient* means
   a. widespread.
   b. slow to recover.
   c. quick to recover.

5 retrospect
(rĕ′trə-spĕkt′)
-*noun*

- After hobbling around on her broken foot for a week before seeing a doctor, Mae then needed surgery. In **retrospect**, it's clear she should have gotten help sooner.
- When I took Ms. Klein's writing course, I thought she was too demanding. In **retrospect**, though, I realize that she taught me more than anyone else.

a *In retrospect* means
   a. looking back.
   b. looking for excuses.
   c. looking ahead.

6 rudimentary
(rōō′də-mĕn′tər-ē)
-*adjective*

- A grammar book usually starts with **rudimentary** skills, such as identifying nouns and verbs.
- I'm so used to adding and subtracting on a calculator that I've probably forgotten how to do those **rudimentary** mathematical calculations on my own.

a *Rudimentary* means
   a. basic.
   b. intermediate.
   c. advanced.

7 scoff
(skŏf)
-verb

- Bystanders **scoffed** at the street musician playing a tune on a row of tin cans, but he seemed unaware that people were making fun of him.
- Tony **scoffed** at reports that a hurricane was coming until he saw the winds knocking down trees and overturning cars.

<u>a</u> *Scoff at* means

  a. to ridicule.   b. to watch.   c. to take seriously.

8 squelch
(skwĕlch)
-verb

- My history teacher shot me a dirty look during class when I couldn't quite manage to **squelch** a burp.
- Decades of communism in Eastern Europe didn't **squelch** the desire for freedom. As soon as they could, the people in these countries began to form democracies.

<u>b</u> *Squelch* means

  a. to encourage.   b. to hold back.   c. to release.

9 venerate
(vĕn'ər-āt')
-verb

- The Tlingit Indians **venerate** the wolf and the raven, and their totem poles illustrate stories in praise of these animals.
- The guests at our dean's retirement banquet made it clear that they **venerated** her; when she entered the room, everyone rose.

<u>b</u> *Venerate* means

  a. to pity.   b. to honor.   c. to remember.

10 zealot
(zĕl'ət)
-noun

- Annie, a **zealot** about health, runs a hundred miles a week and never lets a grain of sugar touch her lips.
- The Crusaders were Christian **zealots** during the Middle Ages who left their homes and families and went off to try to capture the Holy Land.

<u>a</u> *Zealot* means

  a. an extremist.   b. an observer.   c. a doubter.

Matching Words with Definitions

Following are definitions of the ten words. Clearly write or print each word next to its definition. The sentences above and on the previous page will help you decide on the meaning of each word.

1. _____*instigate*_____   To bring about by moving others to action; stir up

2. _____*rudimentary*_____   Fundamental; necessary to learn first

3. _____*resilient*_____   Able to recover quickly from harm, illness, or misfortune

4. _____*collaborate*_____   To work together on a project; cooperate in an effort

5. _____*zealot*_____   A person totally devoted to a purpose or cause

6. _____*squelch*_____   To silence or suppress; crush

7. _____*venerate*_____   To respect deeply; revere

8. _____*despondent*_____   Downhearted; hopeless; overwhelmed with sadness

9. _____*retrospect*_____   Reviewing the past; considering past events

10. _____*scoff*_____   To make fun of; mock; refuse to take seriously

CAUTION: Do not go any further until you are sure the above answers are correct. Then you can use the definitions to help you in the following practices. Your goal is eventually to know the words well enough so that you don't need to check the definitions at all.

➤ *Sentence Check 1*

Using the answer line provided, complete each item below with the correct word from the box. Use each word once.

a. **collaborate**	b. **despondent**	c. **instigate**	d. **resilient**	e. **retrospect**
f. **rudimentary**	g. **scoff**	h. **squelch**	i. **venerate**	j. **zealot**

_____ *rudimentary* _____   1. My ability to speak Spanish is ___, but I can at least manage to ask directions or order a meal.

_____ *despondent* _____   2. Jaime was ___ over the death of his dog, his companion for fourteen years.

_____ *instigate* _____   3. The gang leader wasn't present at the robbery himself, but he was the one who had ___(e)d it.

_____ *zealot* _____   4. Dawn is a ___ about banning nuclear weapons. She has walked for miles in protest marches and stood in the rain for hours during demonstrations.

_____ *venerate* _____   5. Mother Teresa, who devoted her life to helping the poor, is ___(e)d by some people as a twentieth-century saint.

_____ *scoff* _____   6. The Cord, in the 1920s, was the first car with front-wheel drive, but in those days most people considered the idea ridiculous and ___(e)d at it.

_____ *collaborate* _____   7. Marie and Pierre Curie ___(e)d on important scientific experiments involving radioactivity.

_____ *squelch* _____   8. Kim's parents nagged her so hard about practicing the piano that they finally ___(e)d any interest she might have had in music.

_____ *retrospect* _____   9. Since I'd like to be a photographer, I can see, in ___, that I would have gained valuable experience if I'd taken pictures for the school newspaper.

_____ *resilient* _____   10. Athletes need to be ___. After a defeat, an individual or a team must be able to come back and fight for victory the next time.

NOTE: Now check your answers to these questions by turning to page 129. Going over the answers carefully will help you prepare for the next two practices, for which answers are not given.

➤ *Sentence Check 2*

Using the answer lines provided, complete each item below with **two** words from the box. Use each word once.

_____ *rudimentary* _____
_____ *collaborate* _____   1–2. Even though their knowledge of carpentry was only ___, the boys ___(e)d on building a treasure chest.

_____ *scoff* _____
_____ *resilient* _____   3–4. "Everyone gets ___(e)d at now and then," Lynn said. "You just have to be ___ enough to bounce back after a facetious° remark."

_____ *venerate* _____
_____ *despondent* _____   5–6. Many people who ___(e)d Dr. Martin Luther King, Jr., were ___ when he was killed, but then courageously vowed to carry on his work.

instigate _____ 7–8. At the time of the American Revolution, many people viewed those

retrospect _____ who ___(e)d the rebellion as troublemakers. In ___, however, we view them as heroes.

squelch _____ 9–10. Being illiterate until the age of 20 didn't ___ George Washington

zealot _____ Carver's spirit. He went on to become a great botanist—and a ___ about using peanuts, from which he made such products as ink, shampoo, and linoleum.

➤ _Final Check:_ Hardly a Loser

Here is a final opportunity for you to strengthen your knowledge of the ten words. First read the following selection carefully. Then fill in each blank with a word from the box at the top of the previous page. (Context clues will help you figure out which word goes in which blank.) Use each word once.

Tom seemed to be a loser born into a long line of losers. His great-grandfather, condemned to death during the Revolutionary War for siding with the British, had fled to Canada. Tom's father, wanted for arrest after he helped (1)_____ _instigate_ _____ a plot to overthrow the Canadian government, had fled back to the United States.

Tom never received even the most (2)_____ _rudimentary_ _____ formal education. During his mere three months of schooling, he stayed at the bottom of his class. The teacher (3)_____ _scoff_ _____(e)d at him, telling him that he was hopelessly stupid.

Tom's first job, selling papers and candy on a train, ended when he accidentally set the baggage car on fire. His second, as a telegraph operator, ended when he was caught sleeping on the job. At 22, he was jobless, penniless, and living in a cellar. Obviously, Tom's youth had not provided the optimum° foundation for success.

Tom, however, didn't allow his situation to be a detriment° or to (4)_____ _squelch_ _____ his hopes. Instead of becoming (5)_____ _despondent_ _____, he was (6)_____ _resilient_ _____ enough to recover from his misfortunes and find another job. He managed, in fact, to save enough money to open a workshop, where he (7)_____ _collaborate_ _____(e)d with an electrical engineer in designing and then selling machines. A (8)_____ _zealot_ _____ when it came to solving mechanical puzzles, Tom worked nearly nonstop, sleeping only about four hours each night.

By the time he was in his 80s, Tom was credited with over a thousand inventions, including the phonograph, light bulb, and motion picture camera. He was also very famous—so much so that he was (9)_____ _venerate_ _____(e)d nationwide as the greatest living American.

In (10)_____ _retrospect_ _____, Thomas Alva Edison wasn't such a loser after all.

Scores	Sentence Check 2 _____%	Final Check _____%

Enter your scores above and in the vocabulary performance chart on the inside back cover of the book.

ambiguous	inane
dissident	juxtapose
embellish	lethargy
fritter	sporadic
inadvertent	subsidize

Ten Words in Context

In the space provided, write the letter of the meaning closest to that of each **boldfaced** word. Use the context of the sentences to help you figure out each word's meaning.

1 **ambiguous**
(ăm-bĭg′yōo-əs)
-adjective

- The portrait known as the "Mona Lisa" is famous for the woman's **ambiguous** expression. Is she smiling or not?
- Lee left an **ambiguous** message on my answering machine: "Meet me at twelve o'clock." I couldn't tell whether he meant noon or midnight.

_a_ *Ambiguous* means
a. unclear.
b. unintentional.
c. unpleasant.

2 **dissident**
(dĭs′ə-dənt)
-noun

- Some **dissidents** in the Catholic church favor such changes as allowing women to be priests and allowing priests to marry.
- In a dictatorship, **dissidents** are not tolerated. People who speak out against the government may be imprisoned or even executed.

_a_ *Dissident* means
a. a rebel.
b. a dishonest person.
c. a foolish person.

3 **embellish**
(ĕm-bĕl′ĭsh)
-verb

- Lauren **embellished** the door of her locker with postcards from her friends and photos of her cats.
- The cover of the biology textbook was **embellished** with a pattern of colorful seashells.

_b_ *Embellish* means
a. to hide.
b. to decorate.
c. to damage.

4 **fritter**
(frĭt′ər)
-verb

- I thought my little sister would **fritter** away her entire allowance on M&M's, but instead of wasting her money, she put it in her piggy bank.
- Vince **fritters** away both his time and his money playing game after game in video arcades.

_c_ *Fritter away* means
a. to earn.
b. to count.
c. to waste.

5 **inadvertent**
(ĭn-ăd-vûr′t′nt)
-adjective

- Alexander Fleming's discovery of penicillin was **inadvertent**. He forgot to cover a dish of bacteria, and some mold got into it. The next day, Fleming found that the mold had killed the bacteria.
- The final draft of Nancy's paper was shorter than the previous version, but this was **inadvertent**. She had accidentally deleted an entire page without realizing it.

_c_ *Inadvertent* means
a. not required.
b. not finished.
c. not intended.

6 **inane**
(ĭn-ān′)
-adjective

- The conversation at the party was **inane**, consisting mainly of foolish comments about whose clothes were the most "awesome."
- Television programming is often so **inane** that TV has been described as "bubble gum for the mind."

_a_ *Inane* means
a. silly.
b. interesting.
c. shocking.

7 juxtapose
(jŭks′tə-pōz′)
-verb

- The photograph dramatically **juxtaposed** white birch trees and a dark gray sky.
- Dottie spread her new dress out on her bed and then **juxtaposed** all her scarves and jackets to it to see which combination would look best.

_b_ *Juxtapose* means   a. to cover up.   b. to put side by side.   c. to replace.

8 lethargy
(lĕth′ər-jē)
-noun

- Although Wendy seemed to recover from the flu, one symptom persisted—**lethargy**. She felt exhausted for weeks.
- With the hot weather, **lethargy** descended upon the class. The students had trouble staying awake, and even the instructor gazed dreamily out the window.

_a_ *Lethargy* means   a. inactivity.   b. hopelessness.   c. foolishness.

9 sporadic
(spə-răd′ĭk)
-adjective

- It rained continuously until noon. After that, there were only **sporadic** showers.
- Dave makes **sporadic** attempts to give up smoking, but his occasional efforts have been halfhearted.

_b_ *Sporadic* means   a. steady.   b. irregular.   c. long.

10 subsidize
(sŭb′sə-dīz)
-verb

- During college, many students are **subsidized** by their parents, while others rely on grants or loans.
- Public television is **subsidized** by various grants and by individual and community donations.

_a_ *Subsidize* means   a. to pay for.   b. to advertise.   c. to criticize.

Matching Words with Definitions

Following are definitions of the ten words. Clearly write or print each word next to its definition. The sentences above and on the previous page will help you decide on the meaning of each word.

1. ___juxtapose___   To place close together, especially in order to compare or contrast

2. ___lethargy___   A great lack of energy; inactivity due to laziness

3. ___ambiguous___   Able to be interpreted in more than one way; not clear

4. ___inane___   Without sense or meaning; foolish

5. ___dissident___   A person opposed to established ideas or beliefs, especially in politics or religion

6. ___embellish___   To decorate; beautify by adding details

7. ___subsidize___   To support financially; provide a grant or contribution

8. ___fritter___   To spend or waste a little at a time

9. ___inadvertent___   Unintentional; accidental

10. ___sporadic___   Happening now and then; occasional

CAUTION: Do not go any further until you are sure the above answers are correct. Then you can use the definitions to help you in the following practices. Your goal is eventually to know the words well enough so that you don't need to check the definitions at all.

➤ *Sentence Check 1*

Using the answer line provided, complete each item below with the correct word from the box. Use each word once.

a. **ambiguous**	b. **dissident**	c. **embellish**	d. **fritter**	e. **inadvertent**
f. **inane**	g. **juxtapose**	h. **lethargy**	i. **sporadic**	j. **subsidize**

_____ *lethargy* _____ 1. Instead of refreshing me, an afternoon nap only deepens my ___; I wake up even sleepier than I was before.

_____ *sporadic* _____ 2. I get news of Darren only now and then, in ___ letters from him or his mother.

_____ *subsidize* _____ 3. A research grant will ___ Belinda's study of common fears among the elderly.

_____ *inadvertent* _____ 4. My recent trip to Newark was ___. I got on the wrong train.

_____ *fritter* _____ 5. Tracy has learned the hard way not to ___ away her time and affection on friends who don't really care about her in return.

_____ *embellish* _____ 6. My little brother has ___(e)d his bedroom ceiling with stars arranged like several of the constellations.

_____ *juxtapose* _____ 7. In plays and movies, good and evil characters are often ___(e)d. This contrast makes the good ones seem even better and the bad ones seem even worse.

_____ *dissident* _____ 8. When student ___s led a protest against China's communist leaders in 1989, some students were killed by government troops.

_____ *ambiguous* _____ 9. Checking a job applicant's references, the personnel manager was puzzled by one ___ comment: "You will be lucky if you can get her to work for you."

_____ *inane* _____ 10. Steve Martin was poking fun at ___ ideas for products when he said, "I got a fur sink, an electric dog polisher, a gasoline-powered turtleneck sweater—and, of course, I bought some dumb stuff too."

NOTE: Now check your answers to these questions by turning to page 129. Going over the answers carefully will help you prepare for the next two practices, for which answers are not given.

➤ *Sentence Check 2*

Using the answer lines provided, complete each item below with **two** words from the box. Use each word once.

_____ *lethargy* _____ 1–2. "Spring fever" isn't really a detriment° to health, but it often includes
_____ *sporadic* _____ ___: people just want to sleep. Also, attention to work is interrupted off and on by a ___ need to daydream.

_____ *juxtapose* _____ 3–4. On the cover of the news magazine, two pictures were ___(e)d: those of
_____ *dissident* _____ a young ___ and the elderly ruler he was opposing.

_____ *subsidize* _____   5–6. Local businesses ___(e)d our club's Christmas party for the homeless, so we were able to afford a special meal as well as decorations to ___ the room.

_____ *embellish* _____

_____ *fritter* _____   7–8. Why do you want to ___ away your money week after week on tickets for silly movies that all the critics agree are ___?

_____ *inane* _____

_____ *ambiguous* _____   9–10. This week's episode of one television serial had a(n) ___ ending: we don't know whether one of the characters survives his heart attack or dies. In retrospect°, I don't think this was ___. I believe the producers want to keep us guessing so we'll tune in again next week.

_____ *inadvertent* _____

➤ *Final Check:* Grandfather at the Art Museum

Here is a final opportunity for you to strengthen your knowledge of the ten words. First read the following selection carefully. Then fill in each blank with a word from the box at the top of the previous page. (Context clues will help you figure out which word goes in which blank.) Use each word once.

Last Saturday, my grandfather and I spent some time in the modern section of an art museum. Our visit was completely (1)_____ *inadvertent* _____. We'd come to see a show of nature photographs and wandered into the wrong room. Instead of leaving, Grandfather just stood there, staring at the paintings. His idea of worthwhile art is the soft-focus photography on greeting cards, and here was an exhibit of angry paintings by political (2)_____ *dissident* _____s.

In one painting, an empty plate and a plate that was piled high with food had been (3)_____ *juxtapose* _____(e)d on a table; the tablecloth was an American flag. Around this painting was a golden frame that had been (4)_____ *embellish* _____(e)d with tiny plastic models of hot dogs, apple pies, and other typical American foods. There was nothing (5)_____ *ambiguous* _____ about the message—it was crystal-clear. The artist was saying that some people in this country don't have enough to eat. After a few moments of stunned silence, my grandfather jolted the sleepy-looking guard out of his (6)_____ *lethargy* _____ by shouting, "Garbage! What is this garbage?"

When we learned that two major corporations had collaborated° to (7)_____ *subsidize* _____ this exhibit and even owned some of the art works, Grandfather was outraged. "How dare they (8)_____ *fritter* _____ away their money on one piece of unpatriotic trash after another while people are starving?" I tried to explain that the painting itself was a protest against starvation, but Grandfather just scoffed° at me. "Don't be _____ *inane* _____," he said. "Let's get out of here." So we did.

On the way home, Grandfather stared out the car window. He was silent except for (10)_____ *sporadic* _____ sputterings of "Garbage!" and "Incredible!"

| **Scores** | Sentence Check 2 _____% | Final Check _____% |

Enter your scores above and in the vocabulary performance chart on the inside back cover of the book.

berate	maudlin
estrange	regress
euphoric	relinquish
impetuous	ubiquitous
infallible	zenith

Ten Words in Context

In the space provided, write the letter of the meaning closest to that of each **boldfaced** word. Use the context of the sentences to help you figure out each word's meaning.

1 berate
(bē-rāt′)
-verb

- Nick's mother often **berates** him. And when she isn't yelling at him, she ignores him.
- Goldie can accept reasonable criticism, but she was upset when her boss **berated** her loudly in front of everyone else in the office.

_c_ *Berate* means   a. to disappoint.   b. to neglect.   c. to scold angrily.

2 estrange
(ĕ-strānj′)
-verb

- My cousin's recent moodiness has **estranged** some of his old friends.
- After his divorce, Shawn didn't want to **estrange** his children, so he called and visited them often.

_b_ *Estrange* means   a. to frighten.   b. to drive away.   c. to dislike.

3 euphoric
(yōō-fôr′ĭk)
-adjective

- I was **euphoric** when I received my grades. To my amazement and joy, they were all A's and B's.
- Joanne is **euphoric** today, and it's easy to see why she's in such high spirits. She's just gotten the lead role in our school's production of *Beauty and the Beast*.

_a_ *Euphoric* means   a. very happy.   b. boastful.   c. sentimental.

4 impetuous
(ĭm-pĕch′ōō-əs)
-adjective

- Whenever I make an **impetuous** purchase, I end up being dissatisfied: the shoes aren't comfortable, the shirt is the wrong color, the jacket costs too much. From now on, I intend to think more carefully before I buy.
- Children tend to be **impetuous** and often don't think about the consequences of their actions. For instance, they'll throw snowballs at passing cars without worrying about causing an accident.

_a_ *Impetuous* means   a. impulsive.   b. considerate.   c. imaginative.

5 infallible
(ĭn-făl′ə-bəl)
-adjective

- Computers aren't **infallible**. If you put the wrong data into a computer, you'll get wrong answers.
- A sign over my sister's desk reads, "I'm **infallible**. I never make misteaks."

_a_ *Infallible* means   a. perfect.   b. imperfect.   c. everywhere.

6 maudlin
(môd′lĭn)
-adjective

- The verses in greeting cards are often far too sentimental. I prefer humor to such **maudlin** messages.
- The authors of **maudlin** soap operas must feel that they haven't done their job unless viewers are crying by the end of each show.

_c_ *Maudlin* means   a. short.   b. comical.   c. overly emotional.

7 **regress**
(rē-grĕs′)
-*verb*

- When his baby sister was born, seven-year-old Jeremy **regressed** for a while and began sucking his thumb again.
- Adolescents under stress sometimes **regress** to childish ways: dependency, temper tantrums, and silliness.

a *Regress* means   a. to go backward.   b. to reach a high point.   c. to act hastily.

8 **relinquish**
(rĭ-lĭng′kwĭsh)
-*verb*

- No beer is allowed in the "family area" of the stadium, so fans must **relinquish** their six-packs at the gate before they take their seats.
- Donna had to **relinquish** her share in the beach house because she couldn't afford it anymore.

b *Relinquish* means   a. to buy.   b. to yield.   c. to enjoy.

9 **ubiquitous**
(yōō-bĭk′wə-təs)
-*adjective*

- Mites are **ubiquitous**. They live on top of Mt. Everest, in the depths of the ocean, at the South Pole, and even around the roots of your hairs.
- We postponed our plan to drive home on Sunday because a dense fog was **ubiquitous**. It covered the entire town.

c *Ubiquitous* means   a. scarce.   b. newly discovered.   c. found everywhere.

10 **zenith**
(zē′nĭth)
-*noun*

- Florence reached the **zenith** of her career when she became president of Ace Products.
- At age 50, my uncle is afraid that he has already passed the **zenith** of his life; but at age 52, my father thinks the best is yet to come.

c *Zenith* means   a. an end.   b. an earlier condition.   c. the highest point.

Matching Words with Definitions

Following are definitions of the ten words. Clearly write or print each word next to its definition. The sentences above and on the previous page will help you decide on the meaning of each word.

1. *relinquish* — To surrender (something); give (something) up

2. *impetuous* — Done or acting in a hurry, with little thought; impulsive

3. *maudlin* — Tearfully sentimental; overly emotional

4. *berate* — To criticize or scold harshly

5. *ubiquitous* — Existing or seeming to exist everywhere at the same time

6. *zenith* — The highest point or condition; peak

7. *estrange* — To make unsympathetic or unfriendly; alienate

8. *infallible* — Not capable of error or failure; unable to make a mistake

9. *euphoric* — Overjoyed; having an intense feeling of well-being

10. *regress* — To return to an earlier, generally worse, condition or behavior

CAUTION: Do not go any further until you are sure the above answers are correct. Then you can use the definitions to help you in the following practices. Your goal is eventually to know the words well enough so that you don't need to check the definitions at all.

➤ *Sentence Check 1*

Using the answer line provided, complete each item below with the correct word from the box. Use each word once.

| a. **berate** | b. **estrange** | c. **euphoric** | d. **impetuous** | e. **infallible** |
| f. **maudlin** | g. **regress** | h. **relinquish** | i. **ubiquitous** | j. **zenith** |

_____*regress*_____ 1. People in bombed-out, war-torn cities sometimes ___ to more primitive ways of life.

_____*zenith*_____ 2. To many people, Mozart's works represent the ___ of eighteenth-century music.

_____*euphoric*_____ 3. Mei Lin was ___ when the college that was her first choice accepted her.

_____*relinquish*_____ 4. When Dad lost his job, he had to ___ his identification card, his employee parking permit, and the key to his desk.

_____*estrange*_____ 5. Rosina used to be friendly, but since her promotion, she has become so cold that she has ___(e)d former coworkers.

_____*infallible*_____ 6. "I don't expect you to be ___," the boss said, "but I don't want you to make the same mistakes over and over."

_____*berate*_____ 7. "I know I was late," Liz said, "but you could have pointed it out quietly. You didn't have to ___ me."

_____*ubiquitous*_____ 8. In our neighborhood, litter is ___—the sidewalks are ankle-deep in trash. We need a cleanup campaign.

_____*maudlin*_____ 9. Uncle Antonio becomes ___ when he talks about his dear old mother in Italy. And tears also come to the eyes of all who listen.

_____*impetuous*_____ 10. Joyce isn't usually ___, but last week she had a sudden urge to try out her nephew's skateboard. Everyone in the office has already signed the cast on her broken wrist.

NOTE: Now check your answers to these questions by turning to page 129. Going over the answers carefully will help you prepare for the next two practices, for which answers are not given.

➤ *Sentence Check 2*

Using the answer lines provided, complete each item below with **two** words from the box. Use each word once.

_____*infallible*_____
_____*relinquish*_____ 1–2. If people were ___, we could ___ our erasers, our correction tape or fluid, and the "delete" key.

_____*impetuous*_____
_____*berate*_____ 3–4. I'm trying to be less ___, but I still sometimes act on impulse. Later, in retrospect°, I always ___ myself for not using better judgment.

_____*ubiquitous*_____
_____*maudlin*_____ 5–6. Since my father died, reminders of him seem ___. I know I'm being ___, but everywhere I look, I see something that makes me cry.

_____estrange_____ 7–8. Patrick ___(e)d his wife when he wasted their money on gambling and
_____regress_____ ostentatious° clothes. Since their separation, their young daughter has
___(e)d to infantile behavior.

_____zenith_____ 9–10. Our neighborhood basketball team reached its ___ when it won the
_____euphoric_____ citywide championship. The local businesses that had subsidized° the
team were delighted, and the players themselves were ___.

➤ *Final Check:* My Brother's Mental Illness

Here is a final opportunity for you to strengthen your knowledge of the ten words. First read the following selection carefully. Then fill in each blank with a word from the box at the top of the previous page. (Context clues will help you figure out which word goes in which blank.) Use each word once.

My brother Gary is mentally ill. At first my parents thought it was their fault, but now we know that his illness has much more to do with his body chemistry than with anything they did.

Gary's illness involves extreme mood swings. For weeks, he'll be (1)_____euphoric_____, feeling that the world is great and that he's at the (2)_____zenith_____ of life. He may even view himself as (3)_____infallible_____ and get angry if anyone even suggests he has made a mistake. Sometimes, too, he becomes a(n) (4)_____impetuous_____ shopper, spending thousands of dollars on whatever appeals to him. When we ask him to (5)_____relinquish_____ the expensive things he's bought so that we can return them, he refuses, saying he wants to "live like a king." At such times, Gary has to go to the hospital.

Gary's "highs," however, are nothing compared with his "lows." At first, he is simply (6)_____maudlin_____. He may sit in the living room all evening, talking and crying about his former girlfriends, our dead grandmother, or childhood hurts. Misfortune and horror, he says, are (7)_____ubiquitous_____ in his life—there's nowhere he can go to avoid them. Within days, he is very despondent° and so overcome with lethargy° that he can't even get out of bed. Shutting out everyone around him, he (8)_____estrange_____s his family and friends. Then he (9)_____berate_____(e)s himself for all the faults he feels he has. Finally, he tries to kill himself. Again, he must go to the hospital.

When Gary takes his medicine, he does very well. He is charming, bright, and full of life. But when he feels good, he soon stops taking his medicine and begins to (10)_____regress_____. Then we know he is headed for another severe mood swing.

I love my brother dearly, but living with him is like being on a roller coaster. For all of our sakes, I wish we could help him more.

| *Scores* | Sentence Check 2 _____% | Final Check _____% |

Enter your scores above and in the vocabulary performance chart on the inside back cover of the book.

CHAPTER

5

equivocate	propensity
fortuitous	reprehensible
impeccable	sham
liaison	solace
predisposed	solicitous

Ten Words in Context

In the space provided, write the letter of the meaning closest to that of each **boldfaced** word. Use the context of the sentences to help you figure out each word's meaning.

1 equivocate
(ē-kwĭv′ə-kāt′)
-verb

- Bob can't get his boss to say whether or not he intends to give him a raise. When Bob asks him, he **equivocates**, saying, "You've been doing good work, Bob."
- Hank doesn't want to come right out and tell Barb he doesn't love her. If she asks, he **equivocates** by telling her something like "You know how I feel."

_b_ *Equivocate* means   a. to be blunt.   b. to be unclear.   c. to deny.

2 fortuitous
(fôr-tōō′ə-təs)
-adjective

- The birth of triplets wasn't entirely **fortuitous**. The mother had taken a fertility drug, which often causes multiple births.
- It was strictly **fortuitous** that Vince found his missing class notes. They happened to drop out of his dictionary when it fell to the floor.

_a_ *Fortuitous* means   a. accidental.   b. predictable.   c. overdue.

3 impeccable
(ĭm-pĕk′ə-bəl)
-adjective

- My aunt always looks stylish but never overdressed. Her taste in clothes is **impeccable**.
- When she auditioned for the play, Julie gave an **impeccable** performance. She read the lines perfectly.

_a_ *Impeccable* means   a. flawless.   b. deceptive.   c. faulty.

4 liaison
(lē′ə-zōn′)
-noun

- The president of the Student Council acts as a **liaison** between the students and the administration.
- Because she is bilingual, Elsa often serves as a **liaison** between the Spanish- and English-speaking personnel in her office.

_c_ *Liaison* means   a. a follower.   b. a caregiver.   c. a link.

5 predisposed
(prē′dĭs-pōzd′)
-adjective

- Terry didn't want to move in the first place, so she was **predisposed** to hate the new apartment.
- As a Mel Gibson fan, I'm **predisposed** to enjoy any movie he stars in.

_b_ *Predisposed* means   a. unlikely.   b. likely.   c. pretending.

6 propensity
(prə-pĕn′sĭ-tē)
-noun

- Because Ivan has a **propensity** to gain weight, he watches what he eats.
- Cheryl is aware of her **propensity** to blab, so she warns her friends not to tell her anything they wouldn't want repeated.

_b_ *Propensity* means   a. a coincidence.   b. a readiness.   c. a concern.

24

7 reprehensible
(rĕp′rĭ-hĕn′sə-bəl)
-adjective

- The Riordans never discipline their son. No matter how **reprehensible** his behavior is, they just say, "Kids will be kids."
- The company's failure to clean up the oil spill was **reprehensible** and drew harsh criticism.

_a_ *Reprehensible* means   a. shameful.   b. misleading.   c. uncertain.

8 sham
(shăm)
-noun

- Karen's apparent affection for Raul is a **sham**. He's rich, and she cares only about his money.
- When the city inspectors came, the restaurant kitchen was sparkling. However, such cleanliness was a **sham**—the place is usually filthy.

_a_ *Sham* means   a. something false.   b. something confusing.   c. something accidental.

9 solace
(sŏl′ĭs)
-noun

- After a family quarrel, Tamara finds **solace** in the privacy and quiet of her own room.
- When I need **solace** because of some upsetting experience, I find that stroking my cat can be very comforting.

_c_ *Solace* means   a. excitement.   b. perfection.   c. relief.

10 solicitous
(sə-lĭs′ə-təs)
-adjective

- The waiter was overly **solicitous**. He kept interrupting our conversation to ask, "Is everything all right here?"
- **Solicitous** toward her elderly neighbor, Marie calls every day to see how he is feeling and if he needs anything.

_b_ *Solicitous* means   a. distant.   b. attentive.   c. patient.

Matching Words with Definitions

Following are definitions of the ten words. Clearly write or print each word next to its definition. The sentences above and on the previous page will help you decide on the meaning of each word.

1. _____propensity_____   A natural preference or tendency
2. _____reprehensible_____   Deserving of blame, criticism, or disapproval
3. _____fortuitous_____   Happening by chance, by accident, or at random; lucky
4. _____solace_____   Comfort in sorrow or misfortune; consolation
5. _____liaison_____   A person who serves as a connection between individuals or groups; a go-between
6. _____equivocate_____   To be deliberately vague in order to mislead
7. _____impeccable_____   Faultless; perfect
8. _____solicitous_____   Showing or expressing concern, care, or attention
9. _____predisposed_____   Tending toward or open to something beforehand
10. _____sham_____   A pretense or counterfeit; something meant to deceive

CAUTION: Do not go any further until you are sure the above answers are correct. Then you can use the definitions to help you in the following practices. Your goal is eventually to know the words well enough so that you don't need to check the definitions at all.

➤ *Sentence Check 1*

Using the answer line provided, complete each item below with the correct word from the box. Use each word once.

a. **equivocate**	b. **fortuitous**	c. **impeccable**	d. **liaison**	e. **predisposed**
f. **propensity**	g. **reprehensible**	h. **sham**	i. **solace**	j. **solicitous**

_____ *solace* _____   1. When my grandmother died, I found ___ in the thought that she had lived a long, happy life.

_____ *impeccable* _____   2. Jan writes at least three drafts of every paper so that the final result will be ___. She wants each assignment to be perfect.

_____ *predisposed* _____   3. The boss is in a rotten mood today, so he's not ___ to tolerate any mistakes.

_____ *solicitous* _____   4. My brother and I are both grown up, but Mom is still ___ about our health. She says, "You'll always be my babies."

_____ *reprehensible* _____   5. Many people consider child abuse such a(n) ___ crime that they think the penalties should be as harsh as possible.

_____ *sham* _____   6. The "going-out-of-business" sale was a ___. A year later, the store was still open.

_____ *propensity* _____   7. It's hard to believe that Stacy, with her ___ for flashy clothes and nightlife, has become a missionary.

_____ *fortuitous* _____   8. Unexpectedly, I ran into a former neighbor who had just started her own business. The ___ meeting led to a summer job offer for me.

_____ *liaison* _____   9. Olive acted as a ___ between her divorced parents, but she finally insisted that they deal with each other directly.

_____ *equivocate* _____   10. The job candidate ___(e)d when he said he'd been "working out West." Actually, he'd been a ski bum for three years.

NOTE: Now check your answers to these questions by turning to page 129. Going over the answers carefully will help you prepare for the next two practices, for which answers are not given.

➤ *Sentence Check 2*

Using the answer lines provided, complete each item below with **two** words from the box. Use each word once.

_____ *propensity* _____
_____ *equivocate* _____   1–2. When Shirley said she was sick of Len's ___ to flirt with other women, he ___(e)d by making an ambiguous° statement: "I promise you'll never catch me flirting again."

_____ *solace* _____
_____ *liaison* _____   3–4. The woman wasn't permitted to visit her husband, a political prisoner, so it gave her some ___ to have a minister act as a ___ between them.

_____ *predisposed* _____
_____ *solicitous* _____   5–6. Even before I met my father's nurse, I was ___ to like her, because I had heard how ___ she was toward him.

_____ *fortuitous* _____

_____ *reprehensible* _____

7–8. It was strictly ___ that no one was killed when the chemical plant exploded. The explosion, however, was no matter of chance, but the result of ___ carelessness on the part of an employee.

_____ *impeccable* _____

_____ *sham* _____

9–10. The artist was in the illegal business of making copies of paintings, then selling them as originals. His work was so ___ that even museum owners didn't realize the paintings were ___s.

➤ *Final Check:* A Phony Friend

Here is a final opportunity for you to strengthen your knowledge of the ten words. First read the following selection carefully. Then fill in each blank with a word from the box at the top of the previous page. (Context clues will help you figure out which word goes in which blank.) Use each word once.

When my grandfather, Henry Altman, died, he left me a large sum of money. This was very surprising because he and my father had become estranged° years before, after a quarrel, and the old man had never even seen me. I was sad that he had died before we could meet.

Soon after the news of my inheritance, a young man named Seth showed up to offer me his sympathy. Seth said he had been a friend of my grandfather's and that when the old man had become ill, he'd asked Seth to act as a (1)_____ *liaison* _____ between himself and the granddaughter he'd never met. "It's too late for Henry," said Seth, "but I think he'd want me to offer you my friendship. In his later years, he regretted his earlier (2)_____ *propensity* _____ to quarrel with his family."

Believing that Seth had been my grandfather's friend made me (3)_____ *predisposed* _____ to like him, and it gave me (4)_____ *solace* _____ to speak to someone who had known my grandfather. Still, I was puzzled because Seth wasn't able to give me much information. For example, when I asked some questions about Grandfather's second wife, Seth seemed to (5)_____ *equivocate* _____, saying, "All I can say is that she was quite a woman." On the other hand, Seth appeared genuinely (6)_____ *solicitous* _____ about my welfare, and his manners were (7)_____ *impeccable* _____. I had never met anyone so perfectly polite.

I really didn't know what to make of him until, one day, I had a(n) (8)_____ *fortuitous* _____ meeting with an old school friend I hadn't seen in years. When I described Seth, my friend looked startled and said, "I know that guy. He's a phony, a complete (9) _____ *sham* _____. He's after the money, and I bet he never even knew your grandfather."

I did some checking and learned that my friend was right: Seth had tricked several other women out of their inheritances. The next time he called, I told him I knew about his (10)_____ *reprehensible* _____ behavior and would notify the police if he ever tried to contact me again.

Scores	Sentence Check 2 _____%	Final Check _____%

Enter your scores above and in the vocabulary performance chart on the inside back cover of the book.

UNIT ONE: *Review*

The box at the right lists twenty-five words from Unit One. Using the clues at the bottom of the page, fill in these words to complete the puzzle that follows.

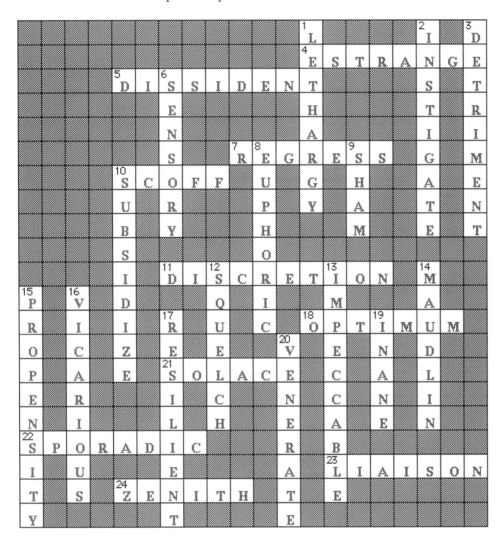

detriment
discretion
dissident
estrange
euphoric
impeccable
inane
instigate
lethargy
liaison
maudlin
optimum
propensity
regress
resilient
scoff
sensory
sham
solace
sporadic
squelch
subsidize
venerate
vicarious
zenith

ACROSS

4. To make unsympathetic or unfriendly; alienate
5. A person opposed to established ideas or beliefs
7. To return to an earlier, generally worse, condition or behavior
10. To make fun of; mock
11. Good judgment or tact in actions or speaking
18. Best possible; most favorable
21. Comfort for sorrow or misfortune; consolation
22. Happening now and then; occasional
23. A person who serves as a connection between individuals or groups
24. The highest point; peak

DOWN

1. A great lack of energy
2. To bring about by moving others to action; stir up
3. Something that causes damage, harm, or loss
6. Having to do with seeing, hearing, feeling, tasting, or smelling
8. Overjoyed; having an intense feeling of well-being
9. A pretense or counterfeit; something meant to deceive
10. To support financially
12. To silence or suppress; crush
13. Faultless; perfect
14. Tearfully sentimental; over-emotional
15. A natural preference or tendency
16. Experienced through the imagination
17. Able to recover quickly from harm, illness, or misfortune
19. Without sense or meaning; foolish
20. To respect deeply; revere

UNIT ONE: Test 1

PART A
Choose the word that best completes each item and write it in the space provided.

_____ _propensity_ _____ 1. When he's caught in a tight spot, Peter has an unfortunate ___ to lie. As a result, few people trust him anymore.

    a. retrospect   b. propensity   c. zenith   d. sham

_____ _venerate_ _____ 2. Asians tend to ___ the elderly, but in America, age does not necessarily bring respect.

    a. berate   b. venerate   c. juxtapose   d. fritter

_____ _instigates_ _____ 3. If Bart's parents leave him alone with his sister for even thirty seconds, he ___ a fight with her.

    a. subsidizes   b. collaborates   c. instigates   d. juxtaposes

_____ _equivocated_ _____ 4. When I asked my father if he liked my new dress, he ___, saying, "That green is a terrific color."

    a. equivocated   b. venerated   c. relinquished   d. collaborated

_____ _sensory_ _____ 5. Our brains interpret our ___ impressions for us. For instance, the images of things we look at must go to the brain so we can actually "see" them.

    a. inadvertent   b. scrupulous   c. sensory   d. resilient

_____ _facetious_ _____ 6. I thought the handyman was being ___ when he said he had to cut a bigger hole in my wall in order to fix the little hole, but that's exactly what he did.

    a. dexterous   b. facetious   c. ubiquitous   d. maudlin

_____ _detriment_ _____ 7. Jaime's shyness may be a ___ to an acting career, in which it helps to be aggressive.

    a. propensity   b. dissident   c. zenith   d. detriment

_____ _squelch_ _____ 8. I tried to ___ the laugh rising in my throat, but seeing the boss looking all over his desk for the glasses he had pushed up on his head was too funny.

    a. squelch   b. venerate   c. berate   d. scoff

_____ _sham_ _____ 9. The invitation we sent my parents to attend a friend's birthday party was a ___. We were actually giving a surprise party in honor of their anniversary.

    a. detriment   b. propensity   c. solace   d. sham

_____ _scrupulous_ _____ 10. Grandfather was known for being ___. Once he spent twenty-five cents for the trolley in order to go back to a store and return the extra nickel that he had received in change.

    a. ambiguous   b. scrupulous   c. vicarious   d. reprehensible

(Continues on next page)

PART B
On the answer line, write the letter of the choice that best completes each item.

____a____ 11. At a party, a **gregarious** person is likely to
      a. be part of a lively group of people.   b. leave early.
      c. sit and talk with just one person all evening.   d. begin an argument over something silly.

____a____ 12. You can consider an event in **retrospect** only
      a. after the event has occurred.   b. before the event happens.
      c. if the event is a happy one.   d. while the event is actually happening.

____c____ 13. Valerie received an unexpected inheritance of $1000. She **frittered** it away by
      a. giving it to her parents to pay household bills.   b. making a down payment on a car.
      c. spending it on clothing and lottery tickets.   d. putting it into her college savings fund.

____b____ 14. A **resilient** person who gets the flu
      a. will probably need a long time to recover.   b. is soon able to resume her normal activities.
      c. complains endlessly about her misfortune.   d. becomes afraid she'll catch something else.

____b____ 15. Some people become downright **maudlin** at weddings. For instance, when my sister got married, Uncle Arthur
      a. refused to kiss the bride.   b. hugged her and sobbed, "You're leaving us!"
      c. seemed quiet and depressed.   d. laughed, told jokes, and danced up a storm.

____a____ 16. Your brother has just announced that he plans to be President someday. You **scoff** at him, saying,
      a. "Right. And I'm going to be the Queen of Sheba."
      b. "That'd be pretty hard, but I bet you could do it."
      c. "Tell me why you are interested in doing that."
      d. "It's cool that you're aiming so high."

____d____ 17. An essay called "How To **Estrange** Your Friends" might suggest
      a. inviting friends to your house to watch videos, eat pizza, and hang out.
      b. offering to teach friends a sport or skill that you're good at.
      c. noticing when friends are feeling depressed and sending them a card or a little gift.
      d. borrowing friends' money and not repaying it.

____d____ 18. You would most likely become **despondent** if
      a. it's a beautiful sunny day, your work is all done, and you've got money in your pocket.
      b. your boss has asked to see you, and you don't know if you're going to be fired or promoted.
      c. the restaurant you went to for lunch was out of your favorite kind of pie.
      d. your best friend is moving away, you've lost your job, and your car has broken down.

____a____ 19. Gene **embellished** his car by
      a. adding fancy hubcaps and a two-tone paint job.
      b. changing the oil at least every three thousand miles.
      c. not getting rid of soda cans and fast-food wrappers.
      d. never having it serviced and letting the engine burn out.

____c____ 20. Keith is known for being **impetuous**. Last week, he
      a. signed up to become a foster parent after thinking about it for several months.
      b. received the "Most Dependable Employee" award at his workplace.
      c. suddenly decided to drive across six states to visit a childhood friend, without even checking to see if the friend was at home.
      d. refused to lend his mother the money she needed to have some emergency dental work done.

Score (Number correct) _____ x 4 = _____%

Enter your score above and in the vocabulary performance chart on the inside back cover of the book.

UNIT ONE: Test 2

PART A
Complete each item with a word from the box. Use each word once.

a. **ambiguous**	b. **euphoric**	c. **infallible**	d. **juxtapose**	e. **lethargy**
f. **predisposed**	g. **regress**	h. **relinquish**	i. **solace**	j. **subsidize**
k. **vicarious**	l. **zealot**	m. **zenith**		

_____zenith_____ 1. Some people who reach the ___ of their careers find that "it's lonely at the top."

_____juxtapose_____ 2. To provide contrast, the photographer ___(e)d the men in their dark suits and the women in their pale dresses.

_____lethargy_____ 3. After a big picnic meal in the warm sun, a(n) ___ came over me, so I took a nap under a sassafras tree.

_____relinquish_____ 4. "If you don't maintain a B average," said the coach, "you ___ your right to be on this team."

_____vicarious_____ 5. Literature and drama allow us to experience problems in a(n) ___ way, giving us painless opportunities to shape our real-life views.

_____subsidize_____ 6. The minister asked business leaders to ___ his Elderly Assistance Program because church donations didn't cover all the costs.

_____euphoric_____ 7. Kay's family was ___ when she arrived home, alive and well, three hours late. She had missed her plane, the one that had crashed.

_____infallible_____ 8. Jason sounds so sure of himself that he gives people the impression he is ___. But he makes mistakes too, just like the rest of us.

_____predisposed_____ 9. Because his father and grandfather both had heart disease, my cousin worries that he may be ___ to the same disorder.

_____solace_____ 10. When the Bakers' young daughter died last year, they found ___ with a support group of other parents who had also lost a child.

_____ambiguous_____ 11. When my older sister asked whether she and her seven kids could visit us for a week, my mother's response was so ___ that I'm not sure if she said yes or no.

_____regress_____ 12. The Bradleys won't go on vacation until their new puppy is fully trained. They're afraid that if he stays at the kennel for a week, he will ___ and start ruining the rugs again.

_____zealot_____ 13. After her first husband died from alcohol-related causes, Carry Nation became an anti-drinking ___. One year, as she crusaded around the country against alcohol, she destroyed twenty saloons with a hatchet.

(Continues on next page)

PART B
Write **C** if the italicized word is used **correctly**. Write **I** if the word is used **incorrectly**.

_I_   14. Sally's appearance was *impeccable*. Even her fingernails were dirty.

_C_   15. A tightrope walker must be both *dexterous* and unafraid of heights.

_C_   16. Theo's behavior toward his sister is *reprehensible*. He shouldn't be allowed to mistreat her so.

_C_   17. In wood shop, we had to learn *rudimentary* skills before we could actually make something.

_I_   18. My aunt and uncle are rich but *ostentatious*. Judging by their modest possessions, you'd never know how much money they really have.

_C_   19. Earth happens to be a place where oxygen is *ubiquitous*, making the planet suitable for many forms of life.

_C_   20. Use *discretion* about where to consult with your doctor. If you run into him or her at church or the supermarket, it's not appropriate to ask about your warts or athlete's foot.

_I_   21. Meeting my brother in the cafeteria at lunchtime was *inadvertent*. We had arranged the night before to meet for lunch.

_I_   22. During my childhood, we made *sporadic* visits to my grandparents' house. Not a Sunday passed that we didn't see them.

_C_   23. As a *liaison* between the hospital staff and patients' families, Jon provides information about patients' conditions in language their families can understand.

_C_   24. I'm not surprised that Lucy is protesting the governor's new welfare policy. She is known for being a *dissident*.

_I_   25. The hotel offers the *optimum* in accommodations. The only guests who ever return there (with friends and relations) are the roaches.

> *Score*   (Number correct) _____ x 4 = _____ %

UNIT ONE: Test 3

PART A: Synonyms
In the space provided, write the letter of the choice that is most nearly the **same** in meaning as the **boldfaced** word.

_c_ 1. **venerate**   a) notice   b) like   c) respect   d) appreciate

_d_ 2. **vicarious**   a) pleasant   b) difficult   c) lively   d) indirect

_a_ 3. **subsidize**   a) support   b) order   c) beautify   d) make unfriendly

_a_ 4. **dexterous**   a) skillful   b) faultless   c) reliable   d) joking

_d_ 5. **sensory**   a) emotional   b) pleasing   c) logical   d) of the senses

_a_ 6. **retrospect**   a) looking back   b) peak   c) waiting   d) prediction

_b_ 7. **embellish**   a) ridicule   b) decorate   c) scold   d) set side by side

_d_ 8. **predisposed**   a) early   b) lucky   c) aware   d) tending toward

_c_ 9. **estrange**   a) give up   b) waste   c) drive away   d) puzzle

_a_ 10. **facetious**   a) humorous   b) sad   c) careless   d) skillful

_d_ 11. **infallible**   a) successful   b) cautious   c) endless   d) faultless

_b_ 12. **discretion**   a) obedience   b) tact   c) imitation   d) goodwill

_c_ 13. **collaborate**   a) decorate   b) stop   c) work together   d) start

_d_ 14. **resilient**   a) showy   b) joyful   c) depressed   d) rapidly recovering

_b_ 15. **juxtapose**   a) work together   b) set side by side   c) imitate   d) avoid the issue

_a_ 16. **fortuitous**   a) accidental   b) planned   c) strong   d) witty

_c_ 17. **impeccable**   a) impossible   b) cautious   c) flawless   d) well-informed

_d_ 18. **dissident**   a) imitator   b) one who doubts   c) supporter   d) protester

_d_ 19. **equivocate**   a) mock   b) become equal   c) begin   d) be purposely vague

_a_ 20. **propensity**   a) tendency   b) talent   c) tact   d) achievement

_b_ 21. **detriment**   a) benefit   b) harm   c) imitation   d) accident

_c_ 22. **zealot**   a) doubter   b) sinner   c) enthusiast   d) impostor

_a_ 23. **sporadic**   a) irregular   b) steady   c) impulsive   d) reliable

_c_ 24. **liaison**   a) tactful   b) pretender   c) connecting link   d) supporter

_b_ 25. **solace**   a) drowsiness   b) comfort   c) friendship   d) misfortune

(Continues on next page)

PART B: Antonyms
In the space provided, write the letter of the choice that is most nearly the **opposite** in meaning to the **boldfaced** word.

_b_ 26. **impetuous**   **a)** sad   **b)** cautious   **c)** rapid   **d)** perfect

_d_ 27. **squander**   **a)** oppose   **b)** respect   **c)** support   **d)** save

_c_ 28. **rudimentary**   **a)** thorough   **b)** unclear   **c)** advanced   **d)** immoral

_a_ 29. **gregarious**   **a)** unsociable   **b)** obedient   **c)** evil   **d)** unknown

_d_ 30. **berate**   **a)** keep   **b)** help   **c)** avoid   **d)** compliment

_a_ 31. **inane**   **a)** sensible   **b)** old   **c)** humorous   **d)** skillful

_b_ 32. **instigate**   **a)** describe   **b)** prevent   **c)** leave   **d)** waste

_d_ 33. **regress**   **a)** choose   **b)** support   **c)** inform   **d)** make progress

_b_ 34. **despondent**   **a)** curious   **b)** happy   **c)** rich   **d)** caring

_c_ 35. **scoff**   **a)** investigate   **b)** offer   **c)** praise   **d)** invite

_a_ 36. **ambiguous**   **a)** clear   **b)** correct   **c)** interesting   **d)** worthwhile

_c_ 37. **reprehensible**   **a)** accidental   **b)** educated   **c)** praiseworthy   **d)** famous

_d_ 38. **inadvertent**   **a)** accurate   **b)** helpful   **c)** serious   **d)** intentional

_c_ 39. **euphoric**   **a)** unfriendly   **b)** modest   **c)** depressed   **d)** curious

_a_ 40. **ostentatious**   **a)** modest   **b)** poor   **c)** sickly   **d)** weak

_d_ 41. **zenith**   **a)** challenge   **b)** young   **c)** average   **d)** bottom

_b_ 42. **scrupulous**   **a)** misinformed   **b)** dishonest   **c)** lazy   **d)** rich

_a_ 43. **relinquish**   **a)** keep   **b)** create   **c)** donate   **d)** prevent

_b_ 44. **solicitous**   **a)** shy   **b)** unconcerned   **c)** sad   **d)** generous

_d_ 45. **sham**   **a)** advantage   **b)** praise   **c)** success   **d)** an original

_b_ 46. **optimum**   **a)** best   **b)** worst   **c)** necessary   **d)** same

_c_ 47. **squelch**   **a)** use   **b)** ridicule   **c)** encourage   **d)** locate

_b_ 48. **lethargy**   **a)** dullness   **b)** liveliness   **c)** relief   **d)** disadvantage

_d_ 49. **maudlin**   **a)** conscientious   **b)** caring   **c)** confident   **d)** unemotional

_b_ 50. **ubiquitous**   **a)** unlucky   **b)** rarely found   **c)** illegal   **d)** moral

Score   (Number correct) _____ x 2 = _____ %

Enter your score above and in the vocabulary performance chart on the inside back cover of the book.

UNIT ONE: Test 4

Each item below starts with a pair of words in CAPITAL LETTERS. For each item, figure out the relationship between these two words. Then decide which of the choices (*a*, *b*, *c*, or *d*) expresses a similar relationship. Write the letter of your choice on the answer line.

_d_ 1. DETRIMENT : ADVANTAGE ::
   a. help : assistance
   c. determination : persistence
   b. work : digging
   d. forgetting : remembering

_a_ 2. DEXTEROUS : BRAIN SURGEON ::
   a. strong : weightlifter
   c. honest : bank robber
   b. young : violinist
   d. neat : mathematician

_b_ 3. GREGARIOUS : UNSOCIABLE ::
   a. ambitious : hardworking
   c. jealous : possessive
   b. enormous : tiny
   d. famous : rich

_a_ 4. OPTIMUM : GOOD ::
   a. worst : bad
   c. careful: careless
   b. best : worse
   d. high : low

_c_ 5. COLLABORATE : TEAMMATES ::
   a. fight : pacifists
   c. compete : rivals
   c. watch : listen
   d. bark : cats

_d_ 6. DESPONDENT : HOPELESS ::
   a. sensible : careless
   c. generous : donation
   b. popular : friendless
   d. fortunate: lucky

_b_ 7. RUDIMENTARY : JELL-O ::
   a. outdated : pudding
   b. expensive : donut
   b. advanced : chocolate souffle
   d. simple : wedding cake

_b_ 8. ZEALOT : SPORTS FAN ::
   a. musician : biologist
   c. scientist : wrestler
   b. athlete : runner
   d. writer : reader

_a_ 9. AMBIGUOUS : MISUNDERSTAND ::
   a. funny : laugh
   c. boring : enjoy
   b. doubtful : agree
   d. clear : disagree

_d_ 10. DISSIDENT : SUPPORT ::
   a. customer : pay
   c. actor : comedy
   b. soprano : sing
   d. leader : follow

(Continues on next page)

_b_ 11. EMBELLISH : COLORED LIGHTS ::

    a. exercise : armchair

    c. eat : nails

              b. destroy : dynamite

              d. sign : scissors

_a_ 12. INANE : SENSELESS ::

    a. injured : hurt

    c. flawed : perfect

              b. pleasing : flower

              d. audible : odorless

_d_ 13. BERATE : NAUGHTY CHILD ::

    a. comfort : lottery winner

    c. obey : prisoner

              b. congratulate : grieving widow

              d. praise : hardworking student

_c_ 14. EUPHORIC : SCHOLARSHIP WINNER ::

    a. calm : bride

    c. frightened : hostage

              b. angry : puppy

              d. surprised : instructor

_a_ 15. IMPETUOUS : CAUTIOUS ::

    a. passionate : unemotional

    c. cheerful : encouraging

              b. quiet : handsome

              d. shy : timid

_d_ 16. UBIQUITOUS : AIR ::

    a. rare : cellular phone

    c. playful : insect

              b. ferocious: giraffe

              d. sparkling : diamond

_c_ 17. FORTUITOUS : BY CHANCE ::

    a. anonymous : by name

    c. commonplace : familiar

              b. blessed : unlucky

              d. automated : by hand

_b_ 18. REPREHENSIBLE : MURDER ::

    a. enjoyable : sickness

    c. impossible : fact

              b. praiseworthy : good deed

              d. terrible : kindness

_a_ 19. SHAM : DISGUISE ::

    a. plan : blueprint

    c. framework : building

              b. smile : frown

              d. mask : face

_b_ 20. SOLICITOUS : UNCARING ::

    a. sole : only

    c. solar : system

              b. satisfying : displeasing

              d. solitary : alone

Score   (Number correct) _____ x 5 = _____%

Enter your score above and in the vocabulary performance chart on the inside back cover of the book.

Unit Two

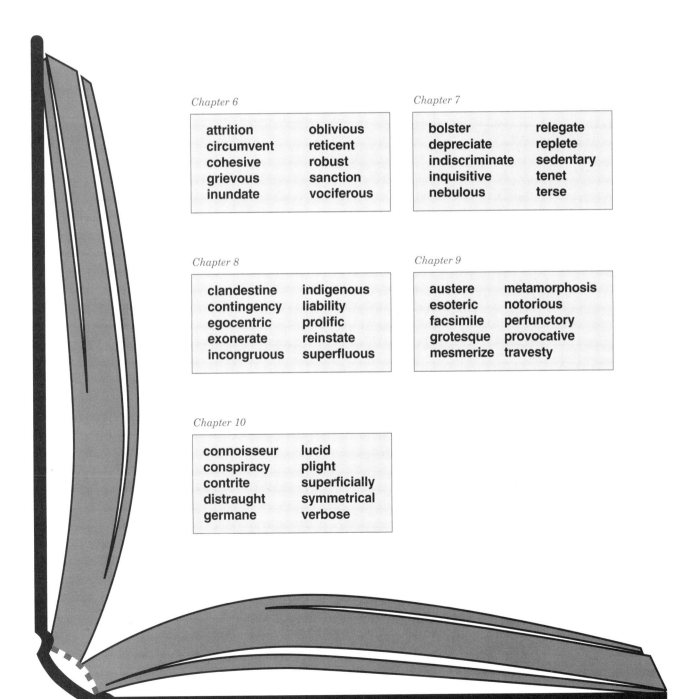

Chapter 6

attrition	oblivious
circumvent	reticent
cohesive	robust
grievous	sanction
inundate	vociferous

Chapter 7

bolster	relegate
depreciate	replete
indiscriminate	sedentary
inquisitive	tenet
nebulous	terse

Chapter 8

clandestine	indigenous
contingency	liability
egocentric	prolific
exonerate	reinstate
incongruous	superfluous

Chapter 9

austere	metamorphosis
esoteric	notorious
facsimile	perfunctory
grotesque	provocative
mesmerize	travesty

Chapter 10

connoisseur	lucid
conspiracy	plight
contrite	superficially
distraught	symmetrical
germane	verbose

attrition	oblivious
circumvent	reticent
cohesive	robust
grievous	sanction
inundate	vociferous

Ten Words in Context

In the space provided, write the letter of the meaning closest to that of each **boldfaced** word. Use the context of the sentences to help you figure out each word's meaning.

1 attrition
(ə-trĭsh′ən)
-*noun*

- Sports teams are constantly looking for new talent to replace players lost through **attrition**—those who retire, quit because of injuries, and so on.
- Colleges try not to have a high rate of **attrition**. They want students to stay until graduation rather than drop out early.

b Attrition means   a. an increase in numbers.   b. a natural loss of individuals.   c. ill health.

2 circumvent
(sŭr′kəm-vĕnt′)
-*verb*

- If we take this roundabout route, we can **circumvent** the rush-hour traffic and get home early.
- I had to swerve to the right to **circumvent** a huge pothole.

a Circumvent means   a. to avoid.   b. to meet head-on.   c. to make smaller.

3 cohesive
(kō-hēs′ĭv)
-*adjective*

- For a **cohesive** pie dough, one that doesn't fall apart, be sure to add enough liquid.
- A family needs to be **cohesive**—to stay together even when stresses and strains threaten to tear it apart.

a Cohesive means   a. connected.   b. popular.   c. large.

4 grievous
(grēv′əs)
-*adjective*

- The death of a beloved pet is a **grievous** loss for a child.
- The assassination of a great leader, such as Mahatma Gandhi or Martin Luther King, Jr., often does **grievous** harm to a society.

c Grievous means   a. preventable.   b. unavoidable.   c. terrible.

5 inundate
(ĭn′ŭn-dāt′)
-*verb*

- During the heavy rains, the river overflowed and **inundated** the fields, destroying all the crops.
- After his brief announcement, the President was **inundated** with questions from reporters.

a Inundate means   a. to flood.   b. to strengthen.   c. to go around.

6 oblivious
(ə-blĭv′ē-əs)
-*adjective*

- The driver continued into the intersection, apparently **oblivious** to the fact that the light had turned red.
- It's easy to spot two people in love. They are the ones who, **oblivious** to everyone else present, see only each other.

b Oblivious to means   a. angry about.   b. not noticing.   c. overwhelmed by.

7 reticent
(rĕt′ə-sənt)
-adjective

- Paul is very **reticent** about his first marriage; he never talks about his former wife or what led to their divorce.
- It's odd that many people who love to gossip about someone else are so **reticent** about their own lives.

_b_ *Reticent* means   a. dishonest.   b. quiet.   c. unaware.

8 robust
(rō-bŭst′)
-adjective

- Once an energetic, **robust** man, Mr. Rand has been considerably weakened by illness.
- A number of weightlifters who were previously **robust** have ruined their health and vigor by taking steroids.

_c_ *Robust* means   a. very noisy.   b. sickly.   c. strong and well.

9 sanction
(săngk′shən)
-verb

- By greeting the dictator with extreme courtesy and fanfare, the legislature seemed to **sanction** his policies.
- Many people whose children attend religious schools would like the government to **sanction** the use of public funds to help pay for their education.

_a_ *Sanction* means   a. to grant approval of.   b. to criticize severely.   c. to remember.

10 vociferous
(vō-sĭf′ər-əs)
-adjective

- When male loons sense that their territory is being invaded, they give **vociferous** cries of challenge.
- The principal became angry and **vociferous**, shouting at students who tried to sneak out of the fire drill.

_c_ *Vociferous* means   a. distant.   b. mild.   c. loud.

Matching Words with Definitions

Following are definitions of the ten words. Clearly write or print each word next to its definition. The sentences above and on the previous page will help you decide on the meaning of each word.

1. _____sanction_____   To authorize, allow, or approve

2. _____inundate_____   To cover, as by flooding; overwhelm with a large number or amount

3. _____circumvent_____   To avoid by going around or as if by going around; to escape from, prevent, or stop through cleverness

4. _____reticent_____   Quiet or uncommunicative; reluctant to speak out

5. _____robust_____   Healthy and strong; vigorous

6. _____cohesive_____   Sticking or holding together; unified

7. _____vociferous_____   Noisy; expressing feelings loudly and intensely

8. _____attrition_____   A gradual natural decrease in number; becoming fewer in number

9. _____grievous_____   Causing grief or pain; very serious or severe

10. _____oblivious_____   Unaware; failing to notice

CAUTION: Do not go any further until you are sure the above answers are correct. Then you can use the definitions to help you in the following practices. Your goal is eventually to know the words well enough so that you don't need to check the definitions at all.

➤ Sentence Check 1

Using the answer line provided, complete each item below with the correct word from the box. Use each word once.

a. **attrition**	b. **circumvent**	c. **cohesive**	d. **grievous**	e. **inundate**
f. **oblivious**	g. **reticent**	h. **robust**	i. **sanction**	j. **vociferous**

_____*oblivious*_____ 1. The chatty, slow-moving clerk at the checkout counter seemed ___ to the fact that the line of impatient customers was growing longer and longer.

_____*vociferous*_____ 2. A quiet, polite discussion may be better than a(n) ___ argument, but some people get more satisfaction out of yelling and shouting.

_____*sanction*_____ 3. In many places, the law doesn't ___ gambling—but the officials don't do much to stop it, either.

_____*robust*_____ 4. A half-hour of aerobic exercise every other day will help you stay ___.

_____*circumvent*_____ 5. People sometimes do odd things to ___ regulations. In New York, when saloons were illegal, one owner called his place "O'Neal's Baloon."

_____*cohesive*_____ 6. If you want your essay to be ___, stick to your point.

_____*grievous*_____ 7. Alzheimer's disease is a disaster for the patient and a(n) ___ burden for the family.

_____*inundate*_____ 8. Some days we're ___(e)d with junk mail—the mailbox is crammed full and overflowing with it.

_____*attrition*_____ 9. The cutting down of the rain forests has caused a dangerous rate of ___ among species that live in those forests.

_____*reticent*_____ 10. Some people who could benefit from counseling avoid seeing a therapist because they are ___ about private matters.

NOTE: Now check your answers to these questions by turning to page 129. Going over the answers carefully will help you prepare for the next two practices, for which answers are not given.

➤ Sentence Check 2

Using the answer lines provided, complete each item below with **two** words from the box. Use each word once.

_____*inundate*_____
_____*oblivious*_____ 1–2. Craig is ___(e)d with bills, but he continues to fritter° away his money. He's ___ to his financial problems.

_____*sanction*_____
_____*attrition*_____ 3–4. The company doesn't ___ the policy of laying off workers. It believes that the optimum° way to reduce the staff is by ___: employees who quit or retire simply aren't replaced.

_____*grievous*_____
_____*reticent*_____ 5–6. Child abuse is a(n) ___ crime, but children are often ___ about it. Their silence may prevent them from cooperating with the police or the courts to bring the abusers to justice.

_____ *robust* _____   7–8. Although my brother was ___ enough to meet the army's standards for

_____ *circumvent* _____   enlisting, his eyesight was too poor. He tried to ___ this problem by memorizing the eye chart.

_____ *vociferous* _____   9–10. The teacher of the Cooking for Health class was ___ about avoiding

_____ *cohesive* _____   egg yolks. "You don't need yolks for a(n) ___ batter!" he shouted. "The whites will hold it together."

➤ *Final Check:* Coco the Gorilla

Here is a final opportunity for you to strengthen your knowledge of the ten words. First read the following selection carefully. Then fill in each blank with a word from the box at the top of the previous page. (Context clues will help you figure out which word goes in which blank.) Use each word once.

Illegal killings of gorillas are reducing their numbers far faster than would be expected from normal (1)_____ *attrition* _____. Here is the story of one gorilla family.

Carrying spears and knives, hunters entered an African game preserve, where it was unlawful to kill or capture wildlife. When they spotted a young gorilla, they closed in. Ten adult gorillas, members of a(n) (2)_____ *cohesive* _____ family group, attempted to shield the infant. The men quickly killed all the adults. As if (3)_____ *oblivious* _____ to the infant's screams, the men strapped his hands and feet to bamboo poles with wire, then carried him down the mountain on which he'd been born.

After several weeks, Dian Fossey, an American studying gorillas in the wild, learned that the young gorilla had been taken to park officials. She found him in a cage so small that he had no room to stand or turn. He was clearly frightened and nearly dead—thirsty, starving, and with infected wounds at his ankles and wrists. Fossey could hardly believe that the officials could (4)_____ *sanction* _____ such reprehensible° cruelty.

When Fossey demanded an explanation from the park's chief official, he seemed (5)_____ *reticent* _____ about the animal. Finally, however, he admitted that he had made an illegal deal with a German zoo. In return for a new car, he had arranged for the gorilla's capture. Fossey was (6)_____ *vociferous* _____ in insisting that the infant be released into her care. The official agreed on the condition that the infant be shipped to the zoo as soon as his health returned.

For several months, Fossey cared for the infant, now named Coco, who would cling to her for comfort. When he became more (7)_____ *robust* _____, he began to romp and explore. In an effort to (8)_____ *circumvent* _____ the agreement to send Coco to the zoo, Fossey (9)_____ *inundate* _____(e)d government officials with letters, begging them to step in and arrange for him to be returned to the wild. In the end, though, the little gorilla was taken away from her—a(n) (10)_____ *grievous* _____ hardship for both of them. Gorillas can live into their 50s, but Coco died in the zoo at the age of 12.

Scores	Sentence Check 2 _____%	Final Check _____%

Enter your scores above and in the vocabulary performance chart on the inside back cover of the book.

bolster	relegate
depreciate	replete
indiscriminate	sedentary
inquisitive	tenet
nebulous	terse

Ten Words in Context

In the space provided, write the letter of the meaning closest to that of each **boldfaced** word. Use the context of the sentences to help you figure out each word's meaning.

1 bolster
(bōl′stər)
-verb

- The front porch was sagging, so we had to **bolster** it with cinder blocks until it could be repaired.
- When Lisa was in the hospital, visits from friends **bolstered** her spirits.

_c_ *Bolster* means   a. to reach.   b. to replace.   c. to support.

2 depreciate
(dĭ-prē′shē-āt′)
-verb

- As soon as you drive a new car off the lot, it **depreciates**; it's immediately worth less than you paid for it.
- The property **depreciated** when the city built a sewage plant nearby.

_b_ *Depreciate* means   a. to become better.   b. to become less valuable.   c. to become definite.

3 indiscriminate
(ĭn′dĭ-skrĭm′ĭ-nĭt)
-adjective

- Some people end up hopelessly in debt because of **indiscriminate** spending, so be selective about what and how much you buy.
- I confess to an **indiscriminate** love of chocolate. I don't distinguish between plain old Hershey bars and fancy imported chocolates—I adore them all.

_c_ *Indiscriminate* means   a. healthy.   b. unenthusiastic.   c. not selective.

4 inquisitive
(ĭn-kwĭz′ə-tĭv)
-adjective

- **Inquisitive** students usually do better than those who are less curious and less eager to learn.
- Small children are naturally **inquisitive**. They wonder about the world around them, and they are constantly asking "Why?"

_c_ *Inquisitive* means   a. hard-working.   b. particular.   c. questioning.

5 nebulous
(nĕb′yə-ləs)
-adjective

- When I ask Leonard what he wants for his birthday, he never gives me any specific ideas. He just gives a **nebulous** answer like "Oh, something I can use."
- "Don't give **nebulous** answers on the exam," said the history instructor. "Be specific."

_a_ *Nebulous* means   a. indefinite.   b. long.   c. specific.

6 relegate
(rĕl′ə-gāt′)
-verb

- At family gatherings, we kids were always **relegated** to the kitchen table while the adults ate in the dining room.
- When we have overnight guests, my parents give them my room and **relegate** me to a cot in the attic.

_a_ *Relegate* means   a. to send.   b. to punish.   c. to reward.

7 replete
(rĭ-plēt′)
-adjective

- The show was **replete** with dazzling effects, including gorgeous scenery, glittering costumes, dramatic lighting, and thrilling music.
- The book of household hints got an excellent review. "It's **replete** with good advice," the critic wrote. "Every homeowner should purchase a copy."

_b_ *Replete* means   a. replaced.   b. filled.   c. followed.

8 sedentary
(sĕd′'n-tĕr′ē)
-adjective

- People in **sedentary** occupations, such as bus drivers and writers, need to make a special effort to exercise.
- My older sister's lifestyle is so **sedentary** that the longest walk she ever takes is from her living room couch to the front seat of her car.

_c_ *Sedentary* means   a. involving much walking.   b. involving stress.   c. involving much sitting.

9 tenet
(tĕn′ĭt)
-noun

- A basic **tenet** of Islam is "There is no God but Allah, and Muhammed is his prophet."
- This world might be a paradise if everyone lived by such **tenets** as "Never cause suffering."

_a_ *Tenet* means   a. a principle.   b. a ritual.   c. a prediction.

10 terse
(tûrs)
-adjective

- I was hurt by Roger's **terse** response to my invitation. All he said was "No thanks."
- A British humor magazine once gave this **terse** advice to people about to marry: "Don't."

_c_ *Terse* means   a. dishonest.   b. unclear.   c. short.

Matching Words with Definitions

Following are definitions of the ten words. Clearly write or print each word next to its definition. The sentences above and on the previous page will help you decide on the meaning of each word.

1. _depreciate_ — To fall or decrease in value or price; to lower the value of

2. _indiscriminate_ — Not chosen carefully; not based on careful selection

3. _sedentary_ — Marked by much sitting; requiring or taking little exercise

4. _tenet_ — A belief or principle held to be true by an individual or group

5. _terse_ — Brief and clear; effectively concise

6. _bolster_ — To hold up, strengthen, or reinforce; support with a rigid object

7. _inquisitive_ — Curious; eager to learn

8. _replete_ — Plentifully supplied; well-filled

9. _nebulous_ — Vague; unclear

10. _relegate_ — To assign to a less important or less satisfying position, place, or condition

CAUTION: Do not go any further until you are sure the above answers are correct. Then you can use the definitions to help you in the following practices. Your goal is eventually to know the words well enough so that you don't need to check the definitions at all.

➤ *Sentence Check 1*

Using the answer line provided, complete each item below with the correct word from the box. Use each word once.

a. **bolster**	b. **depreciate**	c. **indiscriminate**	d. **inquisitive**	e. **nebulous**
f. **relegate**	g. **replete**	h. **sedentary**	i. **tenet**	j. **terse**

terse   1. John considers Arlene rude because her comments are usually ___, but I prefer her brief, clear answers to his long-winded ones.

indiscriminate   2. Pat's TV viewing is ___. He just watches whatever happens to be on.

bolster   3. When a sofa leg broke, we ___(e)d that end of the sofa with a pile of books.

depreciate   4. Houses and antiques often increase in value, but most other things, like cars, computers, and appliances, tend to ___.

tenet   5. A large sign in the boys' treehouse stated their club's main ___: "No Girls or Snakes Allowed!!!"

replete   6. The refrigerator was ___ with all kinds of marvelous foods for the party.

relegate   7. The catcher worried that unless he started playing better, he'd be ___(e)d to the minor leagues.

nebulous   8. Before this semester, my thoughts about a career were ___, but now I have a much clearer idea of what work I want to do.

sedentary   9. When we were children, my active sister was always playing tag or jumping rope. I was more ___, preferring to spend hour after hour just sitting and reading.

inquisitive   10. The book *Answers to 1,001 Interesting Questions* sounds like the perfect gift for a(n) ___ person.

NOTE: Now check your answers to these questions by turning to page 129. Going over the answers carefully will help you prepare for the next two practices, for which answers are not given.

➤ *Sentence Check 2*

Using the answer lines provided, complete each item below with **two** words from the box. Use each word once.

depreciate
nebulous   1–2. When my parents bought their new house, they asked the real estate agent whether it was likely to increase in value or ___. The agent gave this ___ answer: "It's always hard to tell about these things."

relegate
sedentary   3–4. Dad was a construction worker, but as soon as he reached 60—though he was as robust° as ever—his company ___(e)d him to a(n) ___ desk job.

inquisitive
bolster   5–6. The guides at the Leaning Tower of Pisa are inundated° with questions from ___ travelers: "Why is it leaning?" "How far is it leaning?" "Is it being ___(e)d to keep it from falling any further?"

_____ _replete_ _____   7–8. Folk wisdom is ___ with contradictory sayings and ___s. It's fun to
_____ _tenet_ _____   juxtapose° pairs such as "He who hesitates is lost" and "Look before
                                you leap."

_____ _terse_ _____   9–10. Stan is not exactly a ___ speaker, which is why he's earned the
_____ _indiscriminate_ _____   nickname "Motor Mouth." What's more, his conversation is totally
                                ___; he uses no discretion° but just says anything that comes to mind.

➤ _Final Check:_ Our Annual Garage Sale

Here is a final opportunity for you to strengthen your knowledge of the ten words. First read the following selection carefully. Then fill in each blank with a word from the box at the top of the previous page. (Context clues will help you figure out which word goes in which blank.) Use each word once.

It's almost September—time for our annual garage sale. Our unwanted items keep piling up in the basement, which is now so full that we've had to (1)_____ _relegate_ _____ some of the collection to the garage. Though the sale is a lot of work, the sight of all those piles and boxes (2)_____ _bolster_ _____s our determination to go through with it.

This accumulation of stuff has left us with a huge number of possessions for sale, from tools and spools to baskets and gaskets. This year, for example, we have an old bike that some zealot° for exercise might buy and a soft chair and footstool for a more (3)_____ _sedentary_ _____ customer. Our ad states our main (4)_____ _tenet_ _____: "Something for everyone!" Maybe that's a bit (5)_____ _nebulous_ _____, but we don't want to be specific. We just want to communicate the general idea that our sale will be (6)_____ _replete_ _____ with treasures.

Last year, one customer took a quick look and departed with the (7)_____ _terse_ _____ comment "Nothing but junk." However, most people seem to take a completely (8)_____ _indiscriminate_ _____ approach to shopping. They're predisposed° to spend their money on anything, including rusty baking pans and broken lamps. Then there are the (9)_____ _inquisitive_ _____ shoppers who want us to tell them every detail about every item: How old is it? What did we pay for it? Will it increase or (10)_____ _depreciate_ _____ in value?

Friends have foolishly asked us where in the world we get all this junk to sell year after year—an inane° question, because the answer is simple. We shop at garage sales.

Scores	Sentence Check 2 _____%	Final Check _____%

Enter your scores above and in the vocabulary performance chart on the inside back cover of the book.

clandestine	indigenous
contingency	liability
egocentric	prolific
exonerate	reinstate
incongruous	superfluous

Ten Words in Context

In the space provided, write the letter of the meaning closest to that of each **boldfaced** word. Use the context of the sentences to help you figure out each word's meaning.

1 clandestine
(klăn-dĕs′tĭn)
-*adjective*

- In a **clandestine** meeting in an alley, Steve sold his employer's valuable anti-aging formula to a competitor.
- The famous "Underground Railroad" was not an actual railroad; it was a **clandestine** network that took escaped slaves to safety in the years before the Civil War.

_c_ *Clandestine* means   a. popular.   b. unnecessary.   c. concealed.

2 contingency
(kən-tĭn′jən-sē)
-*noun*

- Faye thought her company might transfer her to another city. With that **contingency** in mind, she decided to rent a house rather than buy one.
- We believe in providing for every **contingency**. We have a list of emergency phone numbers, a first-aid kit, and a box of candles in case of a power failure.

_a_ *Contingency* means   a. a possibility.   b. an advantage.   c. a desire.

3 egocentric
(ē′gō-sĕn′trĭk)
-*adjective*

- Denise is completely **egocentric**. Whatever event takes place, she thinks only of how it will affect her personally.
- "We've talked enough about me," said the **egocentric** author to a friend. "Now let's talk about you. What do you think of my new book?"

_a_ *Egocentric* means   a. self-involved.   b. unselfish.   c. self-educated.

4 exonerate
(ĕg-zŏn′ər-āt′)
-*verb*

- Saul was suspected of robbing a bank, but he was **exonerated** when the hidden camera's photos clearly showed someone else holding up the teller.
- Politicians accused of illegal activities always seem to say the same thing: that they'll be **exonerated** when all the facts are known.

_c_ *Exonerate* means   a. to be harmed.   b. to be found guilty.   c. to be found not guilty.

5 incongruous
(ĭn-kŏng′grōō-əs)
-*adjective*

- The cuckoo lays eggs in other birds' nests. This practice can result in the **incongruous** sight of one large cuckoo chick among several tiny baby robins.
- It wasn't really **incongruous** for a former general to join the peace movement. He had seen the horrors of war.

_a_ *Incongruous* means   a. contradictory.   b. unnecessary.   c. not noticeable.

6 indigenous
(ĭn-dĭj′ə-nəs)
-*adjective*

- Kangaroos are **indigenous** only to Australia. They have never been found living anywhere else in the world.
- Corn was not **indigenous** to Europe, so Europeans had never seen or heard of it until their explorers first reached the New World and found it growing there.

_b_ *Indigenous* means   a. important.   b. native.   c. welcomed.

7 **liability**
(lī′ə-bĭl′ə-tē)
-noun

- My shyness with strangers would be a **liability** in any job that involved meeting the public, such as sales.

- When Juanita returned to school at age 40, she was afraid her age would be a **liability**. Instead, she found that it gave her an advantage over younger students.

_b_ *Liability* means   a. an asset.   b. a handicap.   c. a necessity.

8 **prolific**
(prō-lĭf′ĭk)
-adjective

- Rabbits deserve their reputation for being **prolific**. A female can produce three families each summer.

- Haydn was a **prolific** composer. He wrote, among many other musical works, 104 symphonies.

_a_ *Prolific* means   a. creating abundantly.   b. working secretly.   c. important.

9 **reinstate**
(rē′ĭn-stāt′)
-verb

- Michiko left work for a year to stay home with her new baby. When she returned, she was relieved and happy to be **reinstated** in her former job.

- The college had canceled the course in folklore, but the demand was so great that the class had to be **reinstated**.

_c_ *Reinstate* means   a. to recognize.   b. to appreciate.   c. to put back.

10 **superfluous**
(so͝o-pûr′flo͞o-əs)
-adjective

- In the phrase "rich millionaire," the word *rich* is **superfluous**. All millionaires are rich.

- Lately, business at the store has been so slow that the three clerks have almost nothing to do. Two of them seem **superfluous**.

_a_ *Superfluous* means   a. unnecessary.   b. ordinary.   c. required.

Matching Words with Definitions

Following are definitions of the ten words. Clearly write or print each word next to its definition. The sentences above and on the previous page will help you decide on the meaning of each word.

1. _____liability_____ Something that acts as a disadvantage; a drawback

2. _____clandestine_____ Done in secret; kept hidden

3. _____incongruous_____ Out of place; having parts that are not in harmony or that are inconsistent

4. _____contingency_____ A possible future event that must be prepared for or guarded against; possibility

5. _____indigenous_____ Living, growing, or produced naturally in a particular place; native

6. _____superfluous_____ Beyond what is needed, wanted, or useful; extra

7. _____prolific_____ Producing many works, results, or offspring; fertile

8. _____exonerate_____ To clear of an accusation or charge; prove innocent

9. _____egocentric_____ Self-centered; seeing everything in terms of oneself

10. _____reinstate_____ To restore to a previous position or condition; bring back into being or use

CAUTION: Do not go any further until you are sure the above answers are correct. Then you can use the definitions to help you in the following practices. Your goal is eventually to know the words well enough so that you don't need to check the definitions at all.

➤ *Sentence Check 1*

Using the answer line provided, complete each item below with the correct word from the box. Use each word once.

a. **clandestine**	b. **contingency**	c. **egocentric**	d. **exonerate**	e. **incongruous**
f. **indigenous**	g. **liability**	h. **prolific**	i. **reinstate**	j. **superfluous**

_____incongruous_____ 1. Agnes is only five feet tall, but her boyfriend is six-foot-four. They make a(n) ___-looking couple.

_____reinstate_____ 2. Sharon and Ben have ___(e)d a Jewish family tradition they hadn't observed for years: lighting candles on the Sabbath.

_____liability_____ 3. Bad handwriting isn't a serious ___ in an age of computers.

_____indigenous_____ 4. Here, squirrels are red or gray, but I used to live in a state where black squirrels were ___.

_____contingency_____ 5. Although our city has never been struck by an earthquake, it has emergency plans for just such a ___.

_____exonerate_____ 6. Two students were blamed for starting the fire in the physics lab, but they were ___(e)d when it was found that the cause was faulty electrical equipment.

_____prolific_____ 7. Flies are amazingly ___. Within a five-month breeding period, one female can produce thousands of offspring.

_____clandestine_____ 8. Because a submarine is able to hide underwater, it can be very useful in ___ operations.

_____superfluous_____ 9. "Your writing is too wordy," the teacher had written on my paper. "Eliminate all those ___ words and phrases."

_____egocentric_____ 10. Nancy is so ___ that when I told her my car had been stolen, her only reaction was, "Does this mean you can't drive me to work tomorrow?"

NOTE: Now check your answers to these questions by turning to page 129. Going over the answers carefully will help you prepare for the next two practices, for which answers are not given.

➤ *Sentence Check 2*

Using the answer lines provided, complete each item below with **two** words from the box. Use each word once.

_____incongruous_____
_____indigenous_____
1–2. People who spend Christmas in Florida often find the decorations ___. Santa Clauses, sleighs, reindeer, and fir trees somehow seem ___ to the North and look odd juxtaposed° with palm trees and tropical flowers.

_____exonerate_____
_____reinstate_____
3–4. When a million dollars mysteriously vanished, the company decided to fire its accountant. But he was ___(e)d and ___(e)d in his position when the cause was discovered to be a computer malfunction.

_____ _prolific_ _____   5–6. The ___ author has just come out with her fiftieth novel. Although she

_____ _superfluous_ _____   publishes numerous books, her writing style remains tight, with no ___ words.

_____ _egocentric_ _____   7–8. The foreman is so ___ that he has become a ___ to the company.

_____ _liability_ _____   Concerned only with his own needs, he's oblivious° to the needs of the workers.

_____ _clandestine_ _____   9–10. The ship's captain seemed to be losing his mental balance. Fearing that

_____ _contingency_ _____   he might become completely insane, the crew held a(n) ___ meeting to discuss what to do in that ___.

➤ _Final Check:_ My Large Family

Here is a final opportunity for you to strengthen your knowledge of the ten words. First read the following selection carefully. Then fill in each blank with a word from the box at the top of the previous page. (Context clues will help you figure out which word goes in which blank.) Use each word once.

For many years I didn't realize that my family was larger than normal. That's because enormous families somehow seemed (1)_____ _indigenous_ _____ to our neighborhood. I don't know what made people on our block so (2)_____ _prolific_ _____, but the Harrisons, on one side of us, had nine kids; and the Montoyas, on the other side, had twelve. When Mom said she was going to have her eleventh child, the ten of us wondered if another baby wasn't (3)_____ _superfluous_ _____: one more than necessary. Still, I think we enjoyed one another as much as any family I know. Naturally, we had our battles, but though they were sometimes intense, they never lasted long, and it didn't take much to (4)_____ _reinstate_ _____ yourself in a brother's or a sister's good graces. If nothing else worked, you could always (5)_____ _exonerate_ _____ yourself by blaming whatever had happened on another sibling who wasn't home at the moment. Also, we learned to cooperate. When you have to get along with so many different people, you learn not to be (6)_____ _egocentric_ _____. A self-centered person wouldn't have lasted ten minutes in my home.

Of course, there were times when the size of our family was a (7)_____ _liability_ _____. With all those people around, any kind of (8)_____ _clandestine_ _____ activity was just about impossible—there was simply no place to hide and no way to keep a secret. Our numbers could be a disadvantage to others, as well. Once, a new neighbor, not realizing how many of us there were, offered to take us all for ice cream. With amusement, he watched the (9)_____ _incongruous_ _____ sight of nine children and one toddler trying to squeeze into an ordinary passenger car. Although he obviously hadn't been prepared for such a(n) (10)_____ _contingency_ _____, it didn't squelch° his plans. He just grinned and said, "Okay, we'll go in shifts."

Scores Sentence Check 2 _____%	Final Check _____%

Enter your scores above and in the vocabulary performance chart on the inside back cover of the book.

austere	metamorphosis
esoteric	notorious
facsimile	perfunctory
grotesque	provocative
mesmerize	travesty

Ten Words in Context

In the space provided, write the letter of the meaning closest to that of each **boldfaced** word. Use the context of the sentences to help you figure out each word's meaning.

1 austere
(ô-stîr′)
-*adjective*

- Ms. Stone's appearance was **austere**. She wore plain, quiet clothing with no jewelry, and she never used makeup.
- The walls in Alan's den are white and nearly bare, and his white furniture has simple lines. This **austere** decor gives the room a pleasantly calm mood.

_b_ *Austere* means　　a. very ugly.　　b. very plain.　　c. very youthful.

2 esoteric
(ĕs′ə-tĕr′ĭk)
-*adjective*

- The instruction manuals that come with computer software often use such **esoteric** terms that they seem to be written in a foreign language.
- The poetry of Ezra Pound, filled with references to ancient Greek culture, is too **esoteric** for most readers.

_a_ *Esoteric* means　　a. difficult to understand.　　b. shallow.　　c. unfavorable.

3 facsimile
(făk-sĭm′ə-lē)
-*noun*

- When a **facsimile** of an old Sears-Roebuck catalog was published recently, it became a bestseller. People enjoyed seeing what was for sale a century ago.
- The word *fax* is short for **facsimile**. With a fax machine, you can send a precise image of a document across the country electronically in seconds.

_c_ *Facsimile* means　　a. an original.　　b. a distorted version.　　c. an accurate copy.

4 grotesque
(grō-tĕsk′)
-*adjective*

- Most people found the movie character E.T. adorable, but I thought the little alien was **grotesque**, with its weird combination of babyish features and old, wrinkled skin.
- The clown made **grotesque** faces, squinting his eyes, pulling down the corners of his mouth, and sticking out his tongue.

_a_ *Grotesque* means　　a. strange-looking.　　b. hard to understand.　　c. charming.

5 mesmerize
(mĕz′mə-rīz′)
-*verb*

- The intense eyes of the woman in the photograph **mesmerized** me. I couldn't take my eyes off the picture.
- When driving at night, you can become **mesmerized** by the lines on the road or by other cars' headlights or taillights. To avoid a hypnotic state, keep your eyes moving from front to side to rearview mirror.

_b_ *Mesmerize* means　　a. to amuse.　　b. to fascinate.　　c. to distort.

6 metamorphosis
(mĕt′ə-môr′fĕ-sĭs)
-*noun*

- A caterpillar's transformation into a butterfly is a well-known example of **metamorphosis**.
- In Franz Kafka's famous story "The **Metamorphosis**," a man wakes up on his thirtieth birthday to discover that he has turned into an enormous insect.

_a_ *Metamorphosis* means　　a. a change in form.　　b. a disaster.　　c. a scientific theory.

7 notorious
(nō-tôr′ē-əs)
-*adjective*

- Batman and Robin matched wits with the Joker and the Penguin, who were **notorious** for their evil deeds.
- The local diner is **notorious** for bitter coffee, soggy vegetables, limp salads, and mystery meat.

_a_ *Notorious* means   a. regarded negatively.   b. regarded with curiosity.   c. ignored.

8 perfunctory
(pər-fŭnk′tə-rē)
-*adjective*

- The doctor's examination was **perfunctory**. He seemed to be just going through the motions without taking any interest in the patient.
- Most of the candidates were passionate on the subject of nuclear weapons, but one spoke in a very **perfunctory** way, apparently bored with the topic.

_a_ *Perfunctory* means   a. uninterested.   b. enthusiastic.   c. exaggerated.

9 provocative
(prō-vŏk′ə-tĭv)
-*adjective*

- "A good essay is **provocative**," said our English instructor. "It gets the reader interested and attentive starting with the very first paragraph."
- To arouse the viewers' curiosity, the television ad began with a **provocative** image: a spaceship landing on a baseball field, at home plate.

_c_ *Provocative* means   a. predictable.   b. difficult to understand.   c. attention-getting.

10 travesty
(trăv′ĭs-tē)
-*noun*

- The fraternity skit, a **travesty** of college life, exaggerated and ridiculed many campus activities.
- The musical-comedy version of *Hamlet* was a **travesty**. The critics and audience agreed that it made a mockery of Shakespeare's profound tragedy.

_a_ *Travesty* means   a. a joking, disrespectful imitation.   b. an exact copy.   c. a simple version.

Matching Words with Definitions

Following are definitions of the ten words. Clearly write or print each word next to its definition. The sentences above and on the previous page will help you decide on the meaning of each word.

1.	*mesmerize*	To hypnotize or fascinate; hold spellbound
2.	*metamorphosis*	A great or complete change; transformation
3.	*travesty*	A crude, exaggerated, or ridiculous representation; mockery
4.	*perfunctory*	Done only as a routine, with little care or interest; performed with no interest or enthusiasm
5.	*notorious*	Known widely but unfavorably; having a bad reputation
6.	*provocative*	Tending to arouse interest or curiosity
7.	*facsimile*	An exact copy or reproduction
8.	*esoteric*	Intended for or understood by only a certain group; beyond the understanding of most people
9.	*austere*	Without decoration or luxury; severely simple
10.	*grotesque*	Distorted or strikingly inconsistent in shape, appearance, or manner

CAUTION: Do not go any further until you are sure the above answers are correct. Then you can use the definitions to help you in the following practices. Your goal is eventually to know the words well enough so that you don't need to check the definitions at all.

➤ *Sentence Check 1*

Using the answer line provided, complete each item below with the correct word from the box. Use each word once.

a. **austere**	b. **esoteric**	c. **facsimile**	d. **grotesque**	e. **mesmerize**
f. **metamorphosis**	g. **notorious**	h. **perfunctory**	i. **provocative**	j. **travesty**

_____*travesty*_____ 1. The trial was a ___ of justice because several of the jurors had been bribed.

_____*notorious*_____ 2. King Henry VIII of England was ___ not only for getting married six times, but also for ordering two of his wives executed.

_____*provocative*_____ 3. To capture readers' attention, an author sometimes begins an article with a(n) ___ question, such as, "Which do you think is more dangerous, climbing stairs or parachuting out of an airplane?"

_____*grotesque*_____ 4. In some modern paintings, human figures are distorted into such ___ shapes that it's hard to recognize facial features and body parts.

_____*facsimile*_____ 5. Lining the music school's hallway are framed ___s of handwritten pages of music by great composers.

_____*esoteric*_____ 6. Legal documents are usually worded in such ___ language that most people need a lawyer to translate the "legalese" into plain English.

_____*mesmerize*_____ 7. As I stood looking at the grandfather clock, I became ___(e)d by the shiny pendulum that swung back and forth, back and forth, back and forth.

_____*perfunctory*_____ 8. Usually the therapist showed great interest in her patients, but today she was too worried about her own family to give more than ___ responses.

_____*austere*_____ 9. My sister's dormitory room is rather ___, with cement-block walls and bare floors, but she's made it less stark by hanging colorful posters and adding bright bedspreads and cushions.

_____*Metamorphosis*_____ 10. The magician David Copperfield does a trick called "___." One person is chained and locked in a box. When the box is opened, that person is gone, and someone else is chained there instead.

NOTE: Now check your answers to these questions by turning to page 130. Going over the answers carefully will help you prepare for the next two practices, for which answers are not given.

➤ *Sentence Check 2*

Using the answer lines provided, complete each item below with **two** words from the box. Use each word once.

_____*grotesque*_____
_____*travesty*_____ 1–2. The political cartoon showed the judge as a(n) ___ figure, with a huge belly and a gaping mouth. To me it's unfair— a ___ of journalistic ethics.

_____*notorious*_____
_____*austere*_____ 3–4. The cat burglar in the film, ___ for stealing expensive jewelry, committed all his robberies wearing a(n) ___ outfit: a black T-shirt, plain black pants, black shoes, and black gloves.

provocative

mesmerize

5–6. The novel has a(n) ___ opening scene, in which a young woman and her parrot sneak out of a house on a ladder. The novel goes on to ___ the reader with one spellbinding episode after another.

perfunctory

metamorphosis

7–8. Former principals had made only ___ efforts to rid the school of drugs, but the new principal attacked the problem head-on. As a result, the school has undergone a ___ from "hooked" to "clean."

facsimile

esoteric

9–10. At the jewelers' convention, ___s of several famous gems were on display. I enjoyed seeing them, but I didn't understand the accompanying ___ explanation of the technical methods used to produce the copies.

➤ _Final Check:_ A Costume Party

Here is a final opportunity for you to strengthen your knowledge of the ten words. First read the following selection carefully. Then fill in each blank with a word from the box at the top of the previous page. (Context clues will help you figure out which word goes in which blank.) Use each word once.

On the afternoon of a friend's New Year's Eve costume party, I made only a(n) (1)_____ _perfunctory_ _____ effort to put a costume together. Unenthusiastic about spending much time on this, I wanted to do something as simple as possible, even if the effect would be rather (2)_____ _austere_ _____. I decided on a ghost costume—just a plain sheet with eyeholes cut out. Since all my sheets are green, I had to be the ghost of a frog.

The party began for me with a rather (3)_____ _provocative_ _____ encounter: the door was opened by Julia Roberts, clutching her Best Actress Oscar—or at least a very good (4)_____ _facsimile_ _____ of it. Then, when I went inside, the first men I saw were two (5)_____ _notorious_ _____ pirates, Blackbeard and Captain Hook. I listened in on their conversation, expecting to be (6)_____ _mesmerize_ _____(e)d by fascinating tales of cut-throat adventures; instead I heard only the (7)_____ _esoteric_ _____ language of two math majors.

Giving up any hope of understanding their remarks, I looked around for my own friends. But their (8)_____ _metamorphosis_ _____ from ordinary people to famous or odd people was so complete that I couldn't recognize anyone. Most of the costumes were in good taste. One, though, struck me as a (9)_____ _travesty_ _____: a person dressed as Abraham Lincoln—a President I venerate° for his character and leadership—was wearing a bull's-eye target, in crude mockery of President Lincoln's assassination. Another person looked frighteningly (10)_____ _grotesque_ _____, with a mouth twisted to one side and three eyes, all of different sizes.

In the course of the evening, I also met Cleopatra, Shakespeare, and Snoopy, among others. I may never again spend time at a gathering replete° with so many celebrities.

Scores	Sentence Check 2 _____%	Final Check _____%

Enter your scores above and in the vocabulary performance chart on the inside back cover of the book.

connoisseur	lucid
conspiracy	plight
contrite	superficially
distraught	symmetrical
germane	verbose

Ten Words in Context

In the space provided, write the letter of the meaning closest to that of each **boldfaced** word. Use the context of the sentences to help you figure out each word's meaning.

1 connoisseur
(kŏn'ə-sûr')
-noun

- My sister is a **connoisseur** of Southern novels. She's read dozens of them, and she knows all about the authors and their different styles.
- Curtis has broad knowledge of French wines—where they are made, when they are at their best, and exactly how each one tastes. He's a true **connoisseur**.

_b_ *Connoisseur* means   a. a doubter.   b. an authority.   c. a leader.

2 conspiracy
(kən-spĭr'ə-sē)
-noun

- The **conspiracy** to overthrow the government was started by two of the premier's own advisors.
- Although only Lee Harvey Oswald was arrested for the assassination of President Kennedy, many believe there was a **conspiracy** to kill the President.

_a_ *Conspiracy* means   a. a plot.   b. an idea.   c. an announcement.

3 contrite
(kən-trīt')
-adjective

- Dolores was especially **contrite** about tearing her sister's dress because she'd borrowed it without permission.
- Judges are often more lenient with offenders who truly regret their crimes. A criminal who seems genuinely **contrite** may get a shorter sentence.

_c_ *Contrite* means   a. angry.   b. confused.   c. sorry.

4 distraught
(dĭ-strôt')
-adjective

- The parents of the little girl who wandered off in the crowded mall were **distraught** until she was found.
- As the snowstorm got worse and worse and his wife still hadn't arrived home from work, Jeff became increasingly **distraught**.

_a_ *Distraught* means   a. anxious.   b. busy.   c. forgetful.

5 germane
(jər-mān')
-adjective

- Stacy went to the law library to look up information that might be **germane** to her client's case.
- It bothered Christine when her new boss asked if she had a boyfriend. That information certainly wasn't **germane** to her work.

_b_ *Germane* means   a. damaging.   b. related.   c. foreign.

6 lucid
(lōō'sĭd)
-adjective

- I usually find computer manuals horribly unclear, but this one is **lucid**.
- The scientist's explanation of the greenhouse effect was so **lucid** that the entire audience was able to grasp it.

_a_ *Lucid* means   a. easy to understand.   b. repetitious.   c. fair to both sides.

7 plight
(plīt′)
-noun

- The **plight** of the homeless can be somewhat relieved by decent shelters.
- There were reports of a cave-in at the mine, but it was too soon to know much about the **plight** of the trapped miners.

_c_ *Plight* means   a. a delayed situation.   b. an unlikely situation.   c. an unfortunate situation.

8 superficially
(soō′pər-fĭsh′əl-lē)
-adverb

- Leah spent a full week studying for the exam. Joyce, however, reviewed **superficially**, flipping through the pages of her textbook an hour before the test.
- This morning, the mechanic was short of time and and inspected my car only **superficially**. He said he'd check it thoroughly later and then give me an estimate.

_b_ *Superficially* means   a. thoroughly.   b. slightly.   c. daily.

9 symmetrical
(sĭ-mĕ′trĭ-kəl)
-adjective

- The children's sandcastle was **symmetrical**, with a wall on each side and a tower and flag at each end.
- No one's face is perfectly **symmetrical**. For example, one eye is usually slightly higher than the other, and the left and right sides of the mouth differ.

_c_ *Symmetrical* means   a. unique.   b. beautiful.   c. balanced.

10 verbose
(vər-bōs′)
-adjective

- The **verbose** senator said, "At this point in time, we have an urgent and important need for more monetary funds to declare unconditional war on drugs and combat this evil and harmful situation." The reporter wrote, "The senator said we urgently need more money to fight drugs."
- Gabe is the most **verbose** person I know. He always uses ten words when one would do.

_b_ *Verbose* means   a. loud.   b. wordy.   c. self-important.

Matching Words with Definitions

Following are definitions of the ten words. Clearly write or print each word next to its definition. The sentences above and on the previous page will help you decide on the meaning of each word.

1. _distraught_   Very troubled; distressed
2. _verbose_   Using or containing too many words
3. _superficially_   In an on-the-surface manner; not thoroughly
4. _germane_   Having to do with the issue at hand; relevant
5. _lucid_   Clearly expressed; easily understood
6. _contrite_   Truly sorry for having done wrong; repentant
7. _symmetrical_   Well proportioned; balanced; the same on both sides
8. _connoisseur_   An expert in fine art or in matters of taste
9. _plight_   A situation marked by difficulty, hardship, or misfortune
10. _conspiracy_   A secret plot by two or more people, especially for a harmful or illegal purpose

CAUTION: Do not go any further until you are sure the above answers are correct. Then you can use the definitions to help you in the following practices. Your goal is eventually to know the words well enough so that you don't need to check the definitions at all.

➤ *Sentence Check 1*

Using the answer line provided, complete each item below with the correct word from the box. Use each word once.

a. **connoisseur**	b. **conspiracy**	c. **contrite**	d. **distraught**	e. **germane**
f. **lucid**	g. **plight**	h. **superficially**	i. **symmetrical**	j. **verbose**

_____ *contrite* _____ 1. Claire was truly sorry for having started the argument with Sal. To show how ___ she felt, she sent him a special note of apology.

_____ *plight* _____ 2. Everyone is greatly concerned about the ___ of the hostages. We're not even certain they're still alive.

_____ *symmetrical* _____ 3. The garden is ___, with the same flowers and shrubs, arranged in the same pattern, on each side of a central path.

_____ *connoisseur* _____ 4. A ___ of Asian art told me that my Chinese vase is very old, quite rare, and valuable.

_____ *verbose* _____ 5. In writing, it is actually easier to be ___ than to make the effort to cut out the unnecessary words.

_____ *conspiracy* _____ 6. During the Revolutionary War, Benedict Arnold, an American officer, was involved in a ___ to help the British win.

_____ *germane* _____ 7. The teacher and the other students became irritated when Susan kept asking questions that weren't ___ to the class discussion.

_____ *distraught* _____ 8. My parents had expected my sister home by ten o'clock. By the time she finally walked in at two in the morning, they were very ___.

_____ *lucid* _____ 9. Ved's teacher was so pleased with his clear explanation of a difficult theory that she wrote on his paper, "Wonderfully ___!"

_____ *superficially* _____ 10. Whenever Kim tries to buy a new dress, her husband is only ___ interested. If she shows him one and asks his opinion, all he says is, "It's fine. Let's buy it and get out of here."

NOTE: Now check your answers to these questions by turning to page 130. Going over the answers carefully will help you prepare for the next two practices, for which answers are not given.

➤ *Sentence Check 2*

Using the answer lines provided, complete each item below with **two** words from the box. Use each word once.

_____ *distraught* _____
_____ *conspiracy* _____ 1–2. In the novel *Rosemary's Baby*, Rosemary becomes more and more ___ as she realizes that her husband and friends are involved in a ___ against her.

_____ *connoisseur* _____
_____ *superficially* _____ 3–4. Ms. Lewis is a ___ of Native American crafts. She can identify the tribe of the artist after examining a necklace or piece of pottery only ___.

_____ *contrite* _____   5–6. The drunk driver is ___ about causing the accident, but his regret won't give Marsha solace° or ease her ___. She is permanently disabled.

_____ *plight* _____

_____ *germane* _____   7–8. The professor said, "It seems ___ to our discussion of the Age of Reason to mention that ___ architecture was typical. Balance was valued—both in art and in the individual."

_____ *symmetrical* _____

_____ *verbose* _____   9–10. Using too many superfluous° words can make something more difficult to understand. Thus if the essay had not been so ___, it would have been more ___.

_____ *lucid* _____

➤ *Final Check:* The Missing Painting

Here is a final opportunity for you to strengthen your knowledge of the ten words. First read the following selection carefully. Then fill in each blank with a word from the box at the top of the previous page. (Context clues will help you figure out which word goes in which blank.) Use each word once.

It wasn't until noon that Daniel Cobb noticed the painting was missing. He immediately became (1)_____ *distraught* _____. As a (2)_____ *connoisseur* _____ of art, he was well aware of the enormous value of the painting—and this was a grievous° loss. He was so upset that when he phoned the police, he could not think or talk clearly enough to give a (3)_____ *lucid* _____ description of his unfortunate (4)_____ *plight* _____. Instead, he found himself rambling so much that he was afraid the police would think he was just a (5)_____ *verbose* _____ old fool.

Nevertheless, the police soon arrived at Cobb's home, which was magnificent—a fine old mansion in a (6)_____ *symmetrical* _____ style, with a row of columns on each side of the front door. Leading the police to the room from which the painting had been taken, Cobb began to explain. "Last night," he said, "my wife and I gave a dinner party for art experts. We showed them our entire collection. I remember that they gave the missing painting special attention. At least, a few of them seemed to look at it more than just (7)_____ *superficially* _____. I can only assume that we are the victims of a (8)_____ *conspiracy* _____. Our guests must have plotted to sneak into the house during the night and take the painting."

As Cobb finished speaking, his wife entered the room, having just returned from town. She was clearly alarmed by the presence of the police. After Cobb quickly explained, however, she started to laugh. "Today's Monday," she finally said.

"I hardly see how that's (9)_____ *germane* _____ to our problem!" her husband responded.

"Remember, we told the Leeworth Art Association it could exhibit the painting today, for its annual show. That's where I've been. I brought the painting there early this morning."

Cobb looked embarrassed but relieved that his guests had been exonerated° by his wife's story. "Accept my sincere apology for having bothered you. I am most (10)_____ *contrite* _____," he said to the police officers. "Please stay and have some lunch."

Scores	Sentence Check 2 _____%	Final Check _____%

Enter your scores above and in the vocabulary performance chart on the inside back cover of the book.

UNIT TWO: Review

The box at the right lists twenty-five words from Unit Two. Using the clues at the bottom of the page, fill in these words to complete the puzzle that follows.

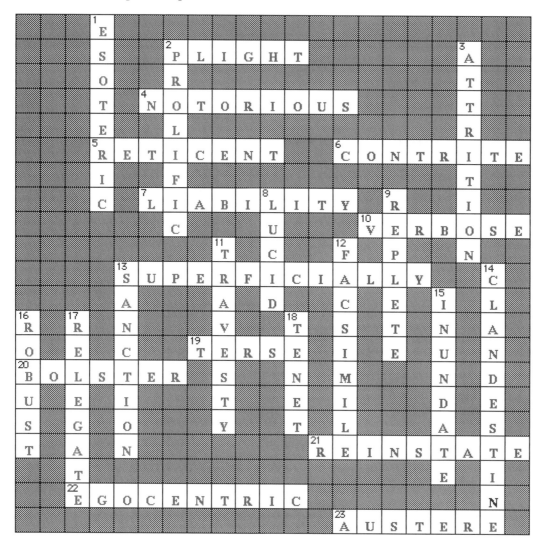

attrition
austere
bolster
clandestine
contrite
egocentric
esoteric
facsimile
inundate
liability
lucid
notorious
plight
prolific
reinstate
relegate
replete
reticent
robust
sanction
superficially
tenet
terse
travesty
verbose

ACROSS

2. A situation marked by difficulty or misfortune
4. Known widely but unfavorably
5. Quiet; reluctant to speak out
6. Truly sorry for having done wrong; repentant
7. Something that acts as a disadvantage; a drawback
10. Using or containing too many words
13. Not thoroughly
19. Brief; clear; concise
20. To support or reinforce
21. To restore to a previous position or condition
22. Self-centered; seeing everything in terms of oneself
23. Without decoration or luxury; severely simple

DOWN

1. Intended for or understood only by a certain group
2. Producing many works, results, or offspring
3. A gradual natural decrease in number
8. Clearly expressed; easily understood
9. Plentifully supplied
11. A crude, exaggerated, or ridiculous representation; a mockery
12. An exact copy
13. To authorize or approve
14. Done in secret; kept hidden
15. To cover, as by flooding; overwhelm with a large number or amount
16. Healthy and strong; vigorous
17. To assign to a less important or less satisfying position
18. A belief or principle held to be true by an individual or group

UNIT TWO: Test 1

PART A

Choose the word that best completes each item and write it in the space provided.

_____cohesive_____ 1. My high-school pals and I were a ___ group. We stuck together through good times and bad.

    a. prolific   b. germane   c. cohesive   d. terse

_____liability_____ 2. In almost any job, being unable to read is a definite ___.

    a. contingency   b. facsimile   c. tenet   d. liability

_____robust_____ 3. Felipe seems so ___ today that it's hard to believe he was close to death only two months ago.

    a. robust   b. terse   c. austere   d. grievous

_____connoisseur_____ 4. Having lived in Italy and studied cooking there, the newspaper's food critic is a ___ of Italian cuisine.

    a. facsimile   b. sanction   c. plight   d. connoisseur

_____notorious_____ 5. New York City drivers are ___ for failing to pay their parking fines. Currently they owe about half a billion dollars.

    a. reticent   b. symmetrical   c. notorious   d. incongruous

_____travesty_____ 6. Some people feel that a circus act in which costumed elephants dance or stand on their heads is a ___ of these intelligent animals' true nature.

    a. liability   b. facsimile   c. conspiracy   d. travesty

_____clandestine_____ 7. Because of the ___ nature of drug dealing, it is very difficult to stop. Most of the transactions take place on dark street corners or behind closed doors.

    a. terse   b. clandestine   c. sedentary   d. inquisitive

_____sanction_____ 8. The managers at Brian's company refused to ___ the early-retirement plan proposed by the union because they felt the plan would cost too much.

    a. relegate   b. sanction   c. inundate   d. circumvent

_____replete_____ 9. A modern American wedding is ___ with customs originally intended to ensure the couple's fertility, including having a wedding cake, throwing rice, and tying shoes to the back of the car.

    a. verbose   b. inquisitive   c. replete   d. grievous

_____grotesque_____ 10. The Englishman John Merrick had an illness that gave him a ___ appearance, which is why he was called "The Elephant Man." Despite people's reactions to his misshapen head and body, Merrick remained affectionate and gentle.

    a. germane   b. superfluous   c. contrite   d. grotesque

(Continues on next page)

PART B

On the answer line, write the letter of the choice that best completes each item.

___d___ 11. Hedda is interested only in **sedentary** jobs, such as
  a. digging ditches.
  b. working in a busy sporting-goods store.
  c. teaching physical-education classes.
  d. sitting at a desk answering an office phone.

___c___ 12. Some people wanted the fired teacher to be **reinstated** because she
  a. didn't deserve her pension.
  b. had already started working at a new job.
  c. was an excellent teacher.
  d. had allowed cheating in her classroom.

___a___ 13. Which of the following phrases contains a **superfluous** word?
  a. "A big huge whale."
  b. "A small red chicken."
  c. "A frisky young dog."
  d. "A beautiful black cat."

___b___ 14. Lilian is extremely **reticent** about her private life. As a result, I
  a. know every detail of her private life.
  b. know almost nothing about it.
  c. really get tired of her bragging.
  d. worry that she trusts the wrong people.

___a___ 15. The **austere** office
  a. had bare walls, a small desk, and one chair.
  b. was filled with desks and file cabinets.
  c. contained fake flowers and cheap posters.
  d. had fine art, live plants, and plush carpets.

___d___ 16. Which of the following is an example of **attrition**?
  a. The number of students enrolled in the algebra class remained the same all semester.
  b. The population in our town has increased so much we've had to build a second school.
  c. In January we had a single pair of mice; by December we had 55 adults and babies.
  d. The 50-year class reunion attracted 47 graduates, while the 60-year reunion of that same class attracted 41 graduates.

___c___ 17. When I came downstairs for breakfast, I saw an **incongruous** sight:
  a. Someone had set the table and made fresh coffee.
  b. All the plates and silverware from dinner were still on the counter, waiting to be washed.
  c. Our cat, normally afraid of water, was curled up in the kitchen sink.
  d. My brother was stirring a pot of oatmeal, which he makes every morning.

___a___ 18. "Let me tell you of my **plight**," the stranger said. "You see,
  a. I've left my wallet in a taxi and I have no money to get home."
  b. I was born in Kansas and my parents were farmers."
  c. I collect rare stamps and coins."
  d. I'd like to offer you a tremendous opportunity to make money."

___c___ 19. The police officer was **superficially** wounded, so the doctor
  a. rushed him to the hospital for immediate surgery.
  b. suggested that he call his family and clergyperson.
  c. put on a bandage and told him he could return to work.
  d. asked to consult with a specialist.

___b___ 20. Because the new morning talk show was not attracting a large audience, it was **relegated** to
  a. 9 p.m., when it could compete with the most popular shows.
  b. 1:30 a.m., when few people would be watching.
  c. an action-adventure series featuring a new kind of danger every week.
  d. a new host with a more sparkling personality.

Score (Number correct) _____ x 4 = _____%

Enter your score above and in the vocabulary performance chart on the inside back cover of the book.

UNIT TWO: Test 2

PART A

Complete each item with a word from the box. Use each word once.

a. **circumvent**	b. **conspiracy**	c. **contrite**	d. **exonerate**	e. **facsimile**
f. **grievous**	g. **inundate**	h. **lucid**	i. **metamorphosis**	j. **oblivious**
k. **prolific**	l. **tenet**	m. **vociferous**		

grievous 1. People who ignore their elderly parents do them a(n) ___ wrong.

lucid 2. Correct punctuation makes prose more ___.

conspiracy 3. The dictator arrested everyone involved in the ___ to overthrow him, including his wife.

facsimile 4. A(n) ___ of a transcript isn't official unless it has been stamped with the seal of the school registrar.

contrite 5. The boys were ___ when they realized that their teasing had made Mary afraid to go to school the next day.

circumvent 6. We tried to ___ the construction area by taking the other highway, but that road was being repaired too.

tenet 7. The main ___ of the "Girls Are Great" club is that girls can do anything boys can do.

exonerate 8. Gerry was accused of stealing a wallet but was ___(e)d when the wallet was found in another student's locker.

oblivious 9. Susan signed in and began work, ___ to the fact that she had forgotten to change from her bedroom slippers into her shoes.

inundate 10. After telling a reader to say goodbye to her boyfriend, the newspaper advice columnist was ___(e)d with thousands of letters saying she was wrong.

vociferous 11. When three-year-old Ginger doesn't get what she wants, her protests are so ___ that you can hear her all over the neighborhood.

metamorphosis 12. After Cristina learned to read at age 30, she underwent a(n) ___. She changed from being shy to being confident, got an interesting new job, and started taking college classes at night.

prolific 13. The most ___ woman on record is a Russian peasant who lived in the early 1700s. She gave birth to sixty-nine children—sixteen pairs of twins, seven sets of triplets, and four sets of quadruplets.

(Continues on next page)

PART B
Write **C** if the italicized word is used **correctly**. Write **I** if the word is used **incorrectly**.

_I_ 14. I was *distraught* when I got the raise I had asked for.

_I_ 15. My uncle is quite *terse*. He talks for at least an hour every time I call him.

_C_ 16. Rose's "How are you?" always seems *perfunctory*, just a matter of routine courtesy, not genuine interest.

_I_ 17. Marsha, as *verbose* as always, signed her letter only "Best," instead of "Best wishes."

_I_ 18. Our bodies are perfectly *symmetrical*—one side is always bigger than the other.

_I_ 19. Some people invest in art and antiques, hoping that their investments will eventually *depreciate*.

_C_ 20. My cousin is so *egocentric* that when the family got together for his sister's graduation, he assumed the gathering was in honor of his new job as manager of a fast-food restaurant.

_C_ 21. The science museum has many *provocative* exhibits, including a giant heart that visitors can walk through.

_I_ 22. Frannie's conversation is so *nebulous* that I always know exactly what she thinks and feels about a subject.

_C_ 23. A tall tree *indigenous* to Australia has been successfully transplanted to the edge of the Sahara Desert, where it keeps the desert from spreading.

_C_ 24. Doris calls herself *inquisitive* because she likes to ask people so many questions, but personally, I think she's just plain nosy.

_C_ 25. The yearbook meeting got sidetracked. Our discussion of our instructors' merits and flaws wasn't *germane* to the topic of the photo layout.

Score   (Number correct) _____ x 4 = _____ %

Enter your score above and in the vocabulary performance chart on the inside back cover of the book.

UNIT TWO: Test 3

PART A: Synonyms

In the space provided, write the letter of the choice that is most nearly the **same** in meaning as the **boldfaced** word.

_d_	1. **terse**	a) organized	b) quiet	c) interesting	d) concise
_a_	2. **plight**	a) difficulty	b) future	c) plot	d) aid
_b_	3. **facsimile**	a) proof	b) copy	c) disadvantage	d) something unusual
_a_	4. **relegate**	a) send to a worse place	b) delay	c) promote	d) leave
_c_	5. **egocentric**	a) self-confident	b) self-taught	c) self-centered	d) selfless
_b_	6. **bolster**	a) question	b) support	c) fix	d) allow
_c_	7. **prolific**	a) successful	b) healthy	c) fertile	d) clear
_b_	8. **notorious**	a) heroic	b) ill-famed	c) vague	d) unaware
_d_	9. **conspiracy**	a) know-how	b) reproduction	c) dilemma	d) plot
_c_	10. **metamorphosis**	a) possibility	b) puzzle	c) change	d) loss
_d_	11. **depreciate**	a) break down	b) forget	c) grow	d) fall in value
_a_	12. **inundate**	a) flood	b) protect	c) visit	d) hypnotize
_b_	13. **contingency**	a) event	b) possibility	c) plan	d) disadvantage
_a_	14. **reinstate**	a) restore	b) find	c) state again	d) select
_c_	15. **inquisitive**	a) unnecessary	b) hard-working	c) questioning	d) difficult
_d_	16. **mesmerize**	a) explain	b) permit	c) confuse	d) fascinate
_a_	17. **circumvent**	a) avoid	b) delay	c) repeat	d) face
_b_	18. **perfunctory**	a) creative	b) routine	c) careful	d) perfect
_c_	19. **attrition**	a) health	b) permission	c) shrinkage	d) addition
_b_	20. **provocative**	a) illegal	b) interesting	c) lawful	d) careless in choosing
_b_	21. **vociferous**	a) unaware	b) noisy	c) serious	d) native
_a_	22. **replete**	a) full	b) supported	c) plain	d) quiet
_b_	23. **tenet**	a) aid	b) principle	c) boarder	d) drawback
_c_	24. **travesty**	a) long journey	b) complete change	c) ridiculous imitation	d) disapproval
_d_	25. **germane**	a) well-known	b) troubled	c) distorted	d) relevant

(Continues on next page)

PART B: Antonyms
In the space provided, write the letter of the choice that is most nearly the **opposite** in meaning to the **boldfaced** word.

___b___ 26. **verbose**   **a)** correct   **b)** concise   **c)** confident   **d)** cautious

___d___ 27. **clandestine**   **a)** legal   **b)** weak   **c)** peaceful   **d)** out in the open

___d___ 28. **liability**   **a)** amusement   **b)** praise   **c)** response   **d)** advantage

___c___ 29. **connoisseur**   **a)** follower   **b)** leader   **c)** beginner   **d)** expert

___b___ 30. **oblivious**   **a)** helpful   **b)** aware   **c)** talkative   **d)** unselfish

___a___ 31. **distraught**   **a)** calm   **b)** factual   **c)** innocent   **d)** unknown

___a___ 32. **grievous**   **a)** pleasing   **b)** famous   **c)** choosy   **d)** careless

___b___ 33. **exonerate**   **a)** admire   **b)** prove guilty   **c)** harm   **d)** support

___c___ 34. **contrite**   **a)** ambitious   **b)** misinformed   **c)** not sorry   **d)** lacking curiosity

___d___ 35. **robust**   **a)** lazy   **b)** dull   **c)** hungry   **d)** weak

___d___ 36. **lucid**   **a)** secret   **b)** shy   **c)** inactive   **d)** unclear

___c___ 37. **superfluous**   **a)** expensive   **b)** common   **c)** necessary   **d)** plain

___a___ ✗ not in book 38. **cursory**   **a)** careful   **b)** blessed   **c)** late   **d)** slow

___c___ 39. **nebulous**   **a)** near   **b)** clever   **c)** clear   **d)** troubled

___b___ 40. **austere**   **a)** loud   **b)** luxurious   **c)** disorganized   **d)** important

___c___ 41. **indiscriminate**   **a)** lucky   **b)** helpful   **c)** choosy   **d)** efficient

___d___ 42. **esoteric**   **a)** famous   **b)** unnecessary   **c)** inexpensive   **d)** widely understood

___c___ 43. **sedentary**   **a)** helpful   **b)** expert   **c)** active   **d)** loud

___b___ (44.) **sanction**   **a)** dislike   **b)** prohibit   **c)** lower in value   **d)** avoid

___b___ 45. **reticent**   **a)** happy   **b)** talkative   **c)** loyal   **d)** having a good reputation

___b___ 46. **incongruous**   **a)** likely   **b)** consistent   **c)** serious   **d)** quiet

___b___ 47. **cohesive**   **a)** routine   **b)** coming apart   **c)** sticking together   **d)** not enough

___c___ 48. **indigenous**   **a)** rich   **b)** poor   **c)** foreign   **d)** legal

___a___ 49. **grotesque**   **a)** well-formed   **b)** caring   **c)** fancy   **d)** uninterested

___c___ 50. **symmetrical**   **a)** irrelevant   **b)** dull   **c)** unbalanced   **d)** ugly

_____

Score   (Number correct) _____ x 2 = _____%

Enter your score above and in the vocabulary performance chart on the inside back cover of the book.

UNIT TWO: Test 4

Each item below starts with a pair of words in CAPITAL LETTERS. For each item, figure out the relationship between these two words. Then decide which of the choices (*a*, *b*, *c*, or *d*) expresses a similar relationship. Write the letter of your choice on the answer line.

_d_ 1. CIRCUMVENT : GO AROUND ::

    a. circulate : stop
    c. bridge : go back

    b. tunnel : go over
    d. depart : go away

_c_ 2. OBLIVIOUS : AWARE ::

    a. obvious : clear
    c. optional : required

    b. insulting : disrespectful
    d. unclear : vague

_d_ 3. RETICENT : SILENT ::

    a. evil : ugly
    c. helpful : nurse

    b. lighthearted : gloomy
    d. well-known : famous

_b_ 4. VOCIFEROUS : PROTESTORS ::

    a. violent : pacifists
    c. virtuous : criminals

    b. brave : heroes
    d. victorious : losers

_c_ 5. BOLSTER : WEAKEN ::

    a. heal : cure
    c. build : destroy

    b. scrub : clean
    d. search : hope

_d_ 6. INDISCRIMINATE : SELECTIVE ::

    a. indistinct : vague
    c. content : satisfied

    b. injurious : harmful
    d. intolerant : open-minded

_c_ 7. SEDENTARY : RECEPTIONIST ::

    a. healthy: plumber
    c. dangerous : firefighter

    b. hammer : carpenter
    d. unskilled : nuclear physicist

_a_ 8. TENET : RELIGION ::

    a. custom : culture
    c. law : friendship

    b. hobby : workplace
    d. foreign policy : day-care center

_d_ 9. CONTINGENCY : PREPARE ::

    a. accident : happen
    c. mistake : intend

    b. car : repair
    d. goal : aim

_a_ 10. EXONERATE : EVIDENCE ::

    a. pollute : chemicals
    c. write : essay

    b. bake : cake
    d. sleep : energy

(Continues on next page)

_c_ 11. INCONGRUOUS : BLUE APPLE ::

    a. unbearable : comfortable   b. inferior : first-class

    c. inedible : granite   d. impossible : somersault

_b_ 12. PROLIFIC : OFFSPRING ::

    a. deceptive : truth   b. imaginative : ideas

    c. children : parents   d. teacher : students

_b_ 13. AUSTERE : PLAIN ::

    a. remote : control   b. nearby : close

    c. strict : easygoing   d. selfish : tantrum

_d_ 14. ESOTERIC : BRAIN SURGERY ::

    a. logical : infancy   c. noisy : sleeping

    b. daring : jogging   d. challenging : mountain climbing

_b_ 15. FACSIMILE : ORIGINAL ::

    a. parent : adult   b. reproduction : painting

    c. brother : man   d. piano : pianist

_a_ 16. MESMERIZE : HYPNOTIST ::

    a. operate : surgeon   b. listen : lecturer

    c. disappear : announcer   d. repair : undertaker

_c_ 17. CONNOISSEUR : TASTE ::

    a. computer programmer : height   b. proofreader : courage

    c. comedian : wit   d. acrobat : clumsiness

_b_ 18. CONSPIRACY : PLOTTERS ::

    a. football field : athletes   b. blueprint : architect

    c. railroad : conductors   d. television : viewers

_c_ 19. SUPERFICIALLY : UNDERSTAND ::

    a. thoroughly : examine   b. slowly : read

    c. briefly : visit   d. race : run

_d_ 20. SYMMETRICAL : SQUARE ::

    a. boxy : circle   b. circular : rectangle

    c. triangular : hoop   d. egg-shaped : oval

Score   (Number correct) _____ x 5 = _____ %

Enter your score above and in the vocabulary performance chart on the inside back cover of the book.

Unit Three

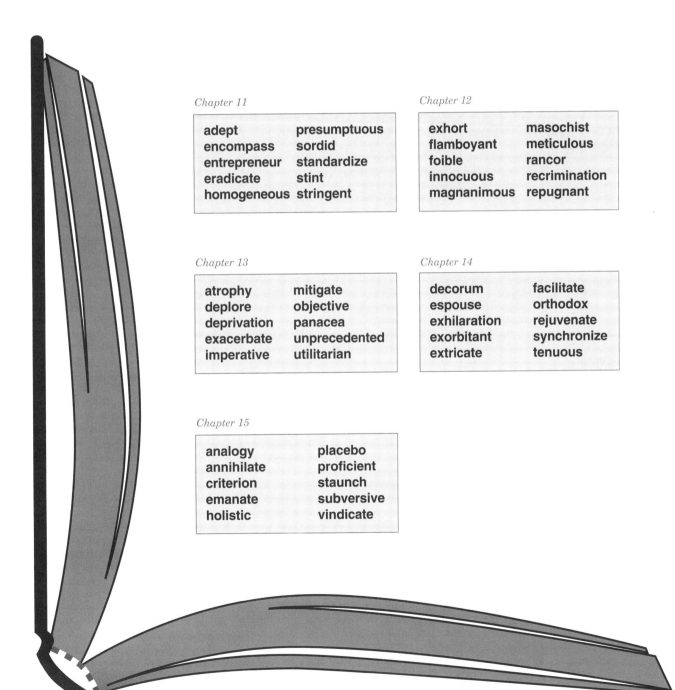

Chapter 11

adept	presumptuous
encompass	sordid
entrepreneur	standardize
eradicate	stint
homogeneous	stringent

Chapter 12

exhort	masochist
flamboyant	meticulous
foible	rancor
innocuous	recrimination
magnanimous	repugnant

Chapter 13

atrophy	mitigate
deplore	objective
deprivation	panacea
exacerbate	unprecedented
imperative	utilitarian

Chapter 14

decorum	facilitate
espouse	orthodox
exhilaration	rejuvenate
exorbitant	synchronize
extricate	tenuous

Chapter 15

analogy	placebo
annihilate	proficient
criterion	staunch
emanate	subversive
holistic	vindicate

CHAPTER 11

adept	**presumptuous**
encompass	**sordid**
entrepreneur	**standardize**
eradicate	**stint**
homogeneous	**stringent**

Ten Words in Context

In the space provided, write the letter of the meaning closest to that of each **boldfaced** word. Use the context of the sentences to help you figure out each word's meaning.

1 adept
(ə-dĕpt')
-adjective

- People enjoy visiting my parents, who are **adept** at making guests feel welcome and at home.
- Justin is an **adept** liar. He always looks so innocent and sincere that everyone believes his lies.

<u>a</u> *Adept* means

    a. skillful.   b. profitable.   c. awkward.

2 encompass
(ĕn-kŭm'pəs)
-verb

- Our history teacher's broad knowledge of the subject **encompasses** details of life in ancient Egypt, Greece, and Rome.
- Tomorrow's test will be difficult because it **encompasses** all the material covered this semester.

<u>c</u> *Encompass* means

    a. to suggest.   b. to omit.   c. to include.

3 entrepreneur
(ŏn'trə-prə-nûr')
-noun

- Glenville has no shopping center, but the city is growing so quickly that smart **entrepreneurs** are sure to start up new businesses there soon.
- My ten-year-old neighbor is already an **entrepreneur**. He set up a lemonade stand last summer and sold homemade cookies at Halloween.

<u>a</u> *Entrepreneur* means

    a. a business investor.   b. an overconfident person.   c. a conformist.

4 eradicate
(ĭ-răd'ĭ-kāt')
-verb

- In recent years, smallpox has been **eradicated**—the first time in history that humans have been able to wipe out a disease. Today many fear the virus may return to the world in the form of biological warfare.
- What makes so many people feel they must **eradicate** all signs of aging? Why should we have to get rid of our wrinkles and gray hair?

<u>c</u> *Eradicate* means

    a. to reveal.   b. to regulate strictly.   c. to erase.

5 homogeneous
(hō'mō-jē'nē-əs)
-adjective

- The student body at Eastman College appears quite **homogeneous**, but there are significant social and economic differences among the students.
- "Homogenized" milk has been made **homogeneous**. This means that it's treated so it will be of uniform consistency, rather than having the cream rise to the top.

<u>b</u> *Homogeneous* means

    a. strictly controlled.   b. the same throughout.   c. of high quality.

6 presumptuous
(prē-zŭmp'chōō-əs)
-adjective

- It was **presumptuous** of Eric to announce his engagement to Phyllis before she had actually agreed to marry him.
- If you ask personal questions at a job interview, you'll be thought **presumptuous**. So, for example, don't ask the interviewer, "What are they paying you?"

<u>a</u> *Presumptuous* means

    a. too forward.   b. skilled.   c. cautious.

7 sordid
(sôr′dĭd)
-*adjective*

• Supermarket tabloids sell well because many people want to know the **sordid** details of celebrities' addictions and messy divorces.

• The reformed criminal now lectures at high schools on how to avoid the mistakes that led him into a **sordid** life as a drug dealer.

_b_ *Sordid* means   a. proud.   b. ugly.   c. natural.

8 standardize
(stăn′dĕr-dīz′)
-*verb*

• When the company **standardized** its pay scale, the salary for each type of job became identical throughout all the departments.

• If Jessica begins selling her homemade soup, she'll have to **standardize** the ingredients. Now she just puts in whatever she has on hand, so the soup is never the same from one day to the next.

_b_ *Standardize* means   a. to do away with.   b. to make consistent.   c. to vary.

9 stint
(stĭnt)
-*noun*

• My **stint** serving hamburgers and fries at a fast-food restaurant convinced me that I needed to get a college degree.

• After traveling during her **stint** in the Navy, Alise wanted a job that would let her continue to see the world.

_a_ *Stint* means   a. an assigned job.   b. a risky undertaking.   c. future work.

10 stringent
(strĭn′jənt)
-*adjective*

• Ms. Jasper has the most **stringent** standards in the department. Passing her course is difficult; getting an A is next to impossible.

• Elected officials should be held to a **stringent** code of ethics, requiring them to avoid even the appearance of wrongdoing.

_c_ *Stringent* means   a. different.   b. flexible.   c. demanding.

Matching Words with Definitions

Following are definitions of the ten words. Clearly write or print each word next to its definition. The sentences above and on the previous page will help you decide on the meaning of each word.

1. _entrepreneur_ — A person who organizes, manages, and takes the risk of a business undertaking
2. _adept_ — Highly skilled; expert
3. _stint_ — A period of work or service
4. _presumptuous_ — Too bold; overly confident
5. _eradicate_ — To get rid of altogether; wipe out
6. _stringent_ — Strictly controlled or enforced; strict; severe
7. _standardize_ — To make uniform; cause to conform to a model
8. _encompass_ — To include; contain
9. _homogeneous_ — Made up of similar or identical parts; uniform throughout
10. _sordid_ — Indecent; morally low; corrupt

CAUTION: Do not go any further until you are sure the above answers are correct. Then you can use the definitions to help you in the following practices. Your goal is eventually to know the words well enough so that you don't need to check the definitions at all.

➤ *Sentence Check 1*

Using the answer line provided, complete each item below with the correct word from the box. Use each word once.

a. **adept**	b. **encompass**	c. **entrepreneur**	d. **eradicate**	e. **homogeneous**
f. **presumptuous**	g. **sordid**	h. **standardize**	i. **stint**	j. **stringent**

_____*presumptuous*_____ 1. It's ___ of Amy to assume she's got the job when others are still being interviewed.

_____*adept*_____ 2. It takes years of study and practice to become ___ at acupuncture.

_____*sordid*_____ 3. In the novel *Oliver Twist*, innocent young Oliver falls into the hands of a gang of pickpockets, who teach him their ___ trade.

_____*stint*_____ 4. My grandfather held many jobs during his life. He even did a(n) ___ as a circus performer.

_____*eradicate*_____ 5. Joyce and Steven's adopted son was abused in an earlier home. They're working hard to ___ the lingering effects on him of that experience.

_____*homogeneous*_____ 6. The town is so close-knit and ___ that newcomers feel out of place. Many of the residents are even related.

_____*encompass*_____ 7. The articles in our small newspaper ___ local and statewide news, but not national or international events.

_____*stringent*_____ 8. My sister applied to several colleges, some with very high admission standards for their students and others with less ___ requirements.

_____*entrepreneur*_____ 9. Doug has just opened an auto repair shop. Now that he's a(n) ___, he can join the National Association for the Self-Employed.

_____*standardize*_____ 10. Should the high school curriculum be ___(e)d throughout the state? Or should each school district be free to design its own courses?

NOTE: Now check your answers to these questions by turning to page 130. Going over the answers carefully will help you prepare for the next two practices, for which answers are not given.

➤ *Sentence Check 2*

Using the answer lines provided, complete each item below with **two** words from the box. Use each word once.

_____*entrepreneur*_____
_____*adept*_____   1–2. To succeed, ___s must be ___ at organization and management. In addition, they must be resilient° enough to deal with the ups and downs of running a business.

_____*stint*_____
_____*stringent*_____   3–4. During Nate's ___ as a teacher at a military academy, he found the rules too ___ for his easygoing, flexible approach.

_____*eradicate*_____
_____*sordid*_____   5–6. After serving a prison term for theft, Charlie is contrite°. He's decided to begin a new life as an honest citizen and ___ all traces of his ___ past.

_____ presumptuous _____
_____ encompass _____

7–8. I've been working at the daycare center only one week, so this suggestion may be ___, but I think the center's program should ___ activities geared to shy children as well as ones for gregarious° kids.

_____ standardize _____
_____ homogeneous _____

9–10. After running the English as a Second Language class a different way every term for a few years, the instructors have finally ___(e)d their approach. On the first night, all students meet as one large class, regardless of their English ability. By the second night, instructors have divided them into smaller, more ___ classes.

➤ Final Check: An Ohio Girl in New York

Here is a final opportunity for you to strengthen your knowledge of the ten words. First read the following selection carefully. Then fill in each blank with a word from the box at the top of the previous page. (Context clues will help you figure out which word goes in which blank.) Use each word once.

Soon after Gina moved from her small Ohio town to New York City, she became so discouraged that she nearly returned home. It was easy to see why she was despondent°: New York had the glamour and excitement that she had expected, but not the high-paying jobs. However, Gina decided to stay in the big city and put in a(n) (1)_____ stint _____ as a waitress in a coffee shop while hoping for something better to turn up. She had been offered only one higher-paying job, as someone who called elderly people and tried to scare them into buying an expensive, unproven "anti-cancer pill," but she felt that this kind of work was too (2)_____ sordid _____.

At least she enjoyed the coffee shop. For someone used to a small, (3)_____ homogeneous _____ town, the customers seemed to come in an enormous variety. Also, the low salary forced her to stick to a(n) (4)_____ stringent _____ budget. As a result of this financial situation, she was becoming (5)_____ adept _____ at making one dollar go as far as two did before.

One day, Gina met a customer who had recently opened a video rental store. This (6)_____ entrepreneur _____ was about to open a second store, and he sometimes discussed his plans with Gina. Although she worried that he might think it (7)_____ presumptuous _____ of a waitress to offer a suggestion about the video business, Gina told him a thought she had about how he might (8)_____ standardize _____ his rental system. He could ask all his customers to fill out the same form. Then a single computer file could (9)_____ encompass _____ all the information. Customers would be signed up automatically for both stores at once. To Gina's relief, the customer didn't scoff° at her idea; in fact, he thanked her for the advice.

Sometime later, he stopped in at the coffee shop to say he needed a capable person to manage his new store. He offered Gina the job. Within a year, she was the manager of three video stores and earning an excellent salary. She was euphoric°, but her happiness would never fully (10)_____ eradicate _____ her memories of those difficult first months in New York.

| Scores | Sentence Check 2 _____% | Final Check _____% |

Enter your scores above and in the vocabulary performance chart on the inside back cover of the book.

exhort	masochist
flamboyant	meticulous
foible	rancor
innocuous	recrimination
magnanimous	repugnant

Ten Words in Context

In the space provided, write the letter of the meaning closest to that of each **boldfaced** word. Use the context of the sentences to help you figure out each word's meaning.

1 exhort
(ĕg-zôrt′)
-verb

- The school counselor gave an impassioned speech to the parents, in which she **exhorted** them to make every effort to keep their children off drugs.
- On the eve of the invasion, the general **exhorted** the troops to fight bravely for their homeland.

_c_ *Exhort* means   a. to accuse.   b. to praise.   c. to urge.

2 flamboyant
(flăm-boi′ənt)
-adjective

- Lily can't resist **flamboyant** clothes. She'd wear a hot-pink dress with gold satin trim to a funeral.
- With his sequined suits, glittering jewelry, and silver piano, Liberace was probably the world's most **flamboyant** pianist.

_a_ *Flamboyant* means   a. flashy.   b. self-centered.   c. concerned with details.

3 foible
(foi′bəl)
-noun

- Serious character flaws—such as abusiveness—are hard to overlook, but **foibles**—such as drinking soup through a straw—can often be easily tolerated.
- "I accept my husband's **foible** of leaving clothes lying around," Barb remarked, "because it lets me be messy without feeling guilty."

_b_ *Foible* means   a. a serious problem.   b. a minor failing.   c. a complaint.

4 innocuous
(ĭn-nŏk′yōō-əs)
-adjective

- Although most children engage in **innocuous** pranks on Halloween, some get out of hand and do serious damage.
- Experts at the Poison Information Center can tell you if a household substance is harmful or **innocuous**.

_a_ *Innocuous* means   a. without bad effects.   b. expensive.   c. satisfying.

5 magnanimous
(măg-năn′ə-məs)
-adjective

- At age 5, Jonathan is already learning to be **magnanimous**. He forgives and hugs his baby sister even when she hits him on the head with a wooden block.
- Last Thanksgiving, someone at work drew a funny picture of our boss as an enormous turkey. When the boss saw it, he was **magnanimous**—he laughed, said it was terrific, and even hung it up over his desk.

_a_ *Magnanimous* means   a. big-hearted.   b. consistent.   c. resentful.

6 masochist
(măs′ə-kĭst)
-noun

- Psychologists are trying to understand why **masochists** obtain satisfaction from suffering.
- "A **masochist's** idea of a good time," said the comedian, "is getting hit by a truck on the way home from having all his teeth pulled."

_b_ *Masochist* means   a. someone filled with hatred.   b. someone who enjoys being hurt.   c. someone who enjoys hurting others.

7 meticulous
(mə-tĭk′yōō-ləs)
-adjective

- When you proofread your own writing, be **meticulous**—check every detail.
- Ken is **meticulous** about his appearance. He never has a wrinkle in his clothing or a hair out of place.

_a_ _Meticulous_ means   a. precise.   b. bold.   c. unconcerned.

8 rancor
(răn′kər)
-noun

- The **rancor** between my uncles has lasted for twenty years, ever since Uncle Dmitri married the woman to whom Uncle Sergei had proposed.
- When there is long-lasting **rancor** between divorced parents, their children may also start to share this bitterness.

_b_ _Rancor_ means   a. a minor fault.   b. deep hostility.   c. secrecy.

9 recrimination
(rĭ-krĭm′ə-nā′shən)
-noun

- The couple's session with the marriage counselor failed miserably; it began with the husband and wife hurling accusations at each other, and it never progressed beyond these **recriminations**.
- When Lainie's father and her teacher met to discuss Lainie's poor grades, they exchanged **recriminations**—each accused the other of not helping her do better.

_c_ _Recrimination_ means   a. an urgent plea.   b. a detailed suggestion.   c. an accusation in reply.

10 repugnant
(rĭ-pŭg′nənt)
-adjective

- My parents find some of my eating habits **repugnant**, but I see nothing offensive about mixing peas and ketchup into mashed potatoes.
- A snake is **repugnant** to many people—"Slimy!" they say, shivering with distaste. However, snakes are not at all slimy, and most are harmless.

_a_ _Repugnant_ means   a. disgusting.   b. amusing.   c. remarkable.

Matching Words with Definitions

Following are definitions of the ten words. Clearly write or print each word next to its definition. The sentences above and on the previous page will help you decide on the meaning of each word.

1. _____rancor_____   Intense hatred or ill will; long-lasting resentment

2. _____innocuous_____   Harmless; inoffensive

3. _____repugnant_____   Offensive; distasteful; repulsive

4. _____masochist_____   A person who gains satisfaction from suffering physical or psychological pain

5. _____flamboyant_____   Very showy; strikingly bold

6. _____foible_____   A minor weakness or character flaw; a minor fault in behavior

7. _____recrimination_____   An accusation made in response to an accuser; countercharge

8. _____exhort_____   To urge with argument or strong advice; plead earnestly

9. _____magnanimous_____   Noble in mind and spirit; especially generous in forgiving

10. _____meticulous_____   Extremely careful and exact; showing great attention to details

CAUTION: Do not go any further until you are sure the above answers are correct. Then you can use the definitions to help you in the following practices. Your goal is eventually to know the words well enough so that you don't need to check the definitions at all.

➤ Sentence Check 1

Using the answer line provided, complete each item below with the correct word from the box. Use each word once.

a. **exhort**	b. **flamboyant**	c. **foible**	d. **innocuous**	e. **magnanimous**
f. **masochist**	g. **meticulous**	h. **rancor**	i. **recrimination**	j. **repugnant**

repugnant   1. Why is it that bats seem so ___? Do we think a flying mouselike creature is distasteful, or do we associate bats with vampires?

magnanimous   2. It was ___ of the Greens to forgive the driver who ran over their dog.

masochist   3. Battered women who stay with their abusive partners aren't necessarily ___s; they don't enjoy being hurt, but often they can't see any way to escape.

foible   4. Although nail-biting is only a ___, it can become maddening to a companion who observes it day after day.

exhort   5. Before the football game, the coach gave a fiery pep talk. He___(e)d the players to fight for the honor of the team and the school.

innocuous   6. To an allergic person, foods that are normally ___, such as milk or wheat, can cause discomfort and even serious illness.

rancor   7. The long-standing ___ between the two women finally came to an end when one of them fell and the other rushed over to help her.

recrimination   8. The angry neighbors traded ___s: "Your wild kids trampled all over my flower bed!" "Well, your crazy dog dug up my lawn!"

meticulous   9. Some jobs needn't be done in a(n) ___ way. For instance, why sweep every speck of dust off a floor that's only going to get dirty again in an hour?

flamboyant   10. On New Year's Day in Philadelphia, string bands called "Mummers" strut their stuff in ___ costumes designed to outshine all other bands in the parade.

NOTE: Now check your answers to these questions by turning to page 130. Going over the answers carefully will help you prepare for the next two practices, for which answers are not given.

➤ Sentence Check 2

Using the answer lines provided, complete each item below with **two** words from the box. Use each word once.

exhort
meticulous   1–2. My second-grade teacher had stringent° standards. For one thing, she ___(e)d us to be ___ about our handwriting. "Dot every *i*," she would say, "and cross every *t*."

rancor
magnanimous   3–4. In a small business, it's important never to instigate° quarrels or let ___ develop. People must learn to be ___ and forgive each other's errors.

masochist
repugnant   5–6. Many find the thought of a ___ seeking out and enjoying suffering to be as ___ as the idea of causing someone else to suffer.

_____*foible*_____   7–8. Walter is certainly odd. Still, most of his ___s—like wearing bedroom
_____*innocuous*_____   slippers to work and leaving bags of pretzels all over the office—are so
___ that nobody really minds them.

_____*recrimination*_____   9–10. When Martha put on a bright red beaded dress with huge rhinestone
_____*flamboyant*_____   earrings, ___s flew back and forth between her and her sister. "You
look ridiculous in that outfit," her sister said. "It's much too ___."
Martha replied, "Well, *your* clothes are the most boring I've ever seen."

➤ *Final Check:* How Neat Is Neat Enough?

Here is a final opportunity for you to strengthen your knowledge of the ten words. First read the following
selection carefully. Then fill in each blank with a word from the box at the top of the previous page.
(Context clues will help you figure out which word goes in which blank.) Use each word once.

Experts say that the most ordinary matters sometimes create the biggest problems in a marriage.
If one spouse is a slob and the other is (1)_____*meticulous*_____, there is bound to be trouble.

At first, newlyweds tend to be (2)_____*magnanimous*_____, readily forgiving each other's
(3)_____*foible*_____s. The wife says it's "sweet" that her husband made the bed while she
was still in it and "cute" that he grabbed her plate to wash it when she picked up her sandwich to
take a bite. "You're so helpful," she coos. And he manages a smile when she dumps her too-
expensive, too-(4)_____*flamboyant*_____ gold sequined dress in the middle of the bedroom
floor. "We've sure got a high-priced, flashy rug," he jokes.

But the honeymoon ends, and the little things that once seemed (5)_____*innocuous*_____ start
to be seriously annoying. He begins to think, "Since my housekeeping is so impeccable°, why isn't
she picking up my good habits? Why must I wade through dirty pantyhose to reach the closet? Why
is there spaghetti sauce on the kitchen ceiling fan again?" He (6)_____*exhort*_____s her to have
some self-respect and stop living like a pig.

And she begins to wonder about him: Why does he insist on dusting the tops of the door
frames when no one can see them? So what if she squeezes the toothpaste from the middle of the
tube—why should he find that harmless habit so (7)_____*repugnant*_____? Maybe he's a
(8)_____*masochist*_____—why else would he be so happy down on his knees, scrubbing the
bathroom floor with a toothbrush (one of the "old" ones that he replaced after using it for a week)?

Soon the accusations and (9)_____*recrimination*_____s start. She yells, "You're a zealot°
for neatness—that's all you care about. You spend more time holding that vacuum cleaner than
you spend holding me!" He responds, "If you weren't so sloppy, I'd hold you more often. As it is,
I have to climb over a mountain of junk just to get near you!"

Eventually, as the two of them continue arguing with each other and berating° each other, their
feelings of (10)_____*rancor*_____ become too great to overcome. It won't be long
before another relationship, so to speak, bites the dust.

Scores	Sentence Check 2 _____%	Final Check _____%

Enter your scores above and in the vocabulary performance chart on the inside back cover of the book.

atrophy	mitigate
deplore	objective
deprivation	panacea
exacerbate	unprecedented
imperative	utilitarian

Ten Words in Context

In the space provided, write the letter of the meaning closest to that of each **boldfaced** word. Use the context of the sentences to help you figure out each word's meaning.

1 atrophy
(ă′trə-fē)
-*verb*

- Since unused muscles **atrophy**, an arm or a leg that remains in a cast for some time becomes thinner.
- "If you watch any more of those mindless television programs," my father said, "your brain will **atrophy**."

 _b_ *Atrophy* means   a. to grow.   b. to waste away.   c. to cause pain.

2 deplore
(dĭ-plôr′)
-*verb*

- Bernie **deplored** his coworkers' habit of taking home paper clips, Scotch tape, pens, and stationery from the office, a practice he felt was dishonest.
- Many people **deplore** some of the content on the Internet but feel they must tolerate it, because they disapprove just as strongly of censorship.

 _a_ *Deplore* means   a. to condemn.   b. to ignore.   c. to make worse.

3 deprivation
(dĕp′rə-vā′shən)
-*noun*

- Children who spend their early years in institutions where they receive no love may suffer throughout life from the effects of this **deprivation**.
- Weight-loss programs typically claim that their members experience no sense of **deprivation**. "You'll never be hungry!" they promise.

 _a_ *Deprivation* means   a. a deficiency.   b. a feeling of disapproval.   c. a strong desire.

4 exacerbate
(ĕg-zăs′ər-bāt)
-*verb*

- Scratching a mosquito bite only makes it worse: the scraping **exacerbates** the itching and may even cause an infection.
- Instead of soothing the baby, the sound of the music box seemed only to **exacerbate** his crying.

 _c_ *Exacerbate* means   a. to find the cause of.   b. to relieve.   c. to make worse.

5 imperative
(ĭm-pĕr′ə-tĭv)
-*adjective*

- It is **imperative** that I renew my driver's license today—it expires at midnight.
- "It is **imperative** for this letter to reach Mr. Rivera tomorrow," the boss said, "so please send it by Express Mail."

 _c_ *Imperative* means   a. impossible.   b. difficult.   c. essential.

6 mitigate
(mĭt′ə-gāt)
-*verb*

- The disabilities resulting from Mr. Dobbs's stroke were **mitigated** by physical therapy, but he still has difficulty using his right arm.
- Time usually **mitigates** the pain of a lost love. When Richard's girlfriend broke their engagement, he was miserable, but now the hurt is much less.

 _a_ *Mitigate* means   a. to relieve.   b. to worsen.   c. to reveal.

7 objective
(əb-jĕk′tĭv)
-adjective

- Scientists must strive to be totally **objective** in their observations and experiments, putting aside their personal wishes and expectations.
- All too often, we let our own prejudices prevent us from being **objective** in judging others.

_b_ *Objective* means   a. personal.   b. open-minded.   c. persuasive.

8 panacea
(păn′ə-sē′ə)
-noun

- My aunt considers vitamins a **panacea**. She believes that they can cure everything from chapped lips to heart disease.
- Ravi thinks his troubles would be over if he just had plenty of money. But money isn't a **panacea**; it wouldn't solve all his problems.

_c_ *Panacea* means   a. a belief.   b. a basic necessity.   c. a universal remedy.

9 unprecedented
(ŭn-prĕs′ə-dĕn′tĭd)
-adjective

- When Sandra Day O'Connor was named to the Supreme Court, her appointment was **unprecedented**—all the previous justices had been men.
- The spring concert was "standing room only." This was **unprecedented**, the first time in our school's history that the concert had been sold out.

_a_ *Unprecedented* means   a. unheard-of.   b. unprejudiced.   c. controversial.

10 utilitarian
(yōō-tĭl′ə-târ′ē-ən)
-adjective

- One difference between "arts" and "crafts" is that crafts tend to be more **utilitarian**. They are generally created to serve a specific use.
- I prefer **utilitarian** gifts, such as pots and pans, to gifts that are meant to be just ornamental or beautiful.

_b_ *Utilitarian* means   a. unique.   b. practical.   c. inexpensive.

Matching Words with Definitions

Following are definitions of the ten words. Clearly write or print each word next to its definition. The sentences above and on the previous page will help you decide on the meaning of each word.

1. _____exacerbate_____   To aggravate (a situation or condition); make more severe

2. _____mitigate_____   To make less severe or less intense; relieve

3. _____unprecedented_____   Being the first instance of something; never having occurred before

4. _____panacea_____   Something supposed to cure all diseases, evils, or difficulties; cure-all

5. _____atrophy_____   To wear down, lose strength, or become weak, as from disuse, disease, or injury (said of a body part); to wither away

6. _____deprivation_____   Lack or shortage of one or more basic necessities

7. _____imperative_____   Necessary; urgent

8. _____objective_____   Not influenced by emotion or personal prejudice; based only on what can be observed

9. _____utilitarian_____   Made or intended for practical use; stressing usefulness over beauty or other considerations

10. _____deplore_____   To feel or express disapproval of

CAUTION: Do not go any further until you are sure the above answers are correct. Then you can use the definitions to help you in the following practices. Your goal is eventually to know the words well enough so that you don't need to check the definitions at all.

➣ *Sentence Check 1*

Using the answer line provided, complete each item below with the correct word from the box. Use each word once.

a. **atrophy**	b. **deplore**	c. **deprivation**	d. **exacerbate**	e. **imperative**
f. **mitigate**	g. **objective**	h. **panacea**	i. **unprecedented**	j. **utilitarian**

deprivation   1. When families go camping and decide to spend a whole weekend without pizza and TV, some kids think they are experiencing a great ___.

mitigate   2. The last time I had a migraine headache, I tried draping a cold, wet cloth over my eyes to ___ the pain and nausea, but they only got worse.

exacerbate   3. First-aid instructions usually advise against moving an accident victim, because movement can ___ an injury.

unprecedented   4. The election of John F. Kennedy, a Catholic, to the presidency was ___ in American history—he was the first Catholic president.

deplore   5. No one could ___ drinking and driving more than Elena; her son was killed by a drunk driver.

utilitarian   6. Although an Academy Award is not meant to be ___, one winner uses his as a paperweight.

objective   7. If you find it difficult to be ___ about your own writing, try asking a classmate to read it and give you an unbiased opinion.

panacea   8. Our city has many different crime-related problems, but the mayor has only one solution to offer: more police officers on the streets. She believes an enlarged police force is a ___.

imperative   9. When told that Ms. Thomas was in conference and could not be disturbed, the caller said urgently, "It's ___ that I speak to her. Her house is on fire."

atrophy   10. In Burma, some women lengthen their necks by stretching them with copper coils. This practice damages the muscles, causing them to ___: they become thin and weak.

NOTE: Now check your answers to these questions by turning to page 130. Going over the answers carefully will help you prepare for the next two practices, for which answers are not given.

➣ *Sentence Check 2*

Using the answer lines provided, complete each item below with **two** words from the box. Use each word once.

mitigate
deprivation   1–2. "Hands Across America" was a fund-raising effort to help ___ hunger in regions where ___ was widespread.

deplore
unprecedented   3–4. Many people are so opposed to change that they ___ as potentially harmful just about anything that is new and ___.

_____ exacerbate _____ 5–6. It's hard to know what treatment is optimum° for a sprained ankle. Walking on the ankle can ___ the injury, but if you don't walk on it for a long time, the muscles will start to ___.
_____ atrophy _____

_____ objective _____ 7–8. If you want to be ___, it is ___ that you put aside your emotions and prejudices.
_____ imperative _____

_____ utilitarian _____ 9–10. In deciding which over-the-counter medicine to take, it's important to use a(n) ___ approach. Choose a drug for the specific purpose it serves, and don't rely on any one drug as a ___.
_____ panacea _____

➤ Final Check: Thomas Dooley

Here is a final opportunity for you to strengthen your knowledge of the ten words. First read the following selection carefully. Then fill in each blank with a word from the box at the top of the previous page. (Context clues will help you figure out which word goes in which blank.) Use each word once.

In the 1950s, a young American doctor named Thomas Dooley arrived in Laos, in southeast Asia. He was shocked by the ubiquitous° sickness and poverty he found there. The people lived without plumbing or electricity, and they had no knowledge of health care or even of basic hygiene. For example, one boy with an infected leg had been told not to walk at all, which caused both of his legs to (1)_____ atrophy _____. The people's lack of knowledge was (2)_____ exacerbate _____(e)d by superstitions and by a reliance on well-meaning traditional healers, who sometimes inadvertently° gave useless or harmful advice. They might, for example, instruct a person to rub pig grease into a burn or treat a fracture by chanting. Dooley (3)_____ deplore _____(e)d the terrible (4)_____ deprivation _____ he saw. He felt that it was (5)_____ imperative _____ to help these communities learn about modern medicine—to help them apply (6)_____ objective _____ scientific knowledge—and equally essential for them to relinquish° their harmful superstitions. Dooley did not believe that modern medicine would be a (7)_____ panacea _____ for every problem in Laos, but he firmly believed that he could at least (8)_____ mitigate _____ the people's suffering.

Dooley's (9)_____ utilitarian _____ approach to health care, based specifically on practical instruction, was (10)_____ unprecedented _____: no one before him had tried to teach the communities how to care for themselves. Dooley believed that teaching was an essential part of medical care, that it was useless to treat symptoms and allow the causes to continue. So, subsidized° by local governments, he set up hospitals and taught the rudimentary° principles of hygiene, nursing, and medical treatment.

Tom Dooley died at a tragically young age, but his work and the tenets° that guided it benefited countless people.

Scores   Sentence Check 2 _____%   Final Check _____%

Enter your scores above and in the vocabulary performance chart on the inside back cover of the book.

decorum	facilitate
espouse	orthodox
exhilaration	rejuvenate
exorbitant	synchronize
extricate	tenuous

Ten Words in Context

In the space provided, write the letter of the meaning closest to that of each **boldfaced** word. Use the context of the sentences to help you figure out each word's meaning.

1 decorum
(dǐ-kô′rəm)
-noun

- **Decorum** demands that you send a thank-you note for all birthday gifts, even those you don't like or will never use.
- In her newspaper columns, Miss Manners gives advice on **decorum** in all kinds of situations. For example, she says that at a dinner party, you must be polite even if you find a bug crawling in your salad.

_c_ *Decorum* means   a. a difficult situation.   b. beauty.   c. proper conduct.

2 espouse
(ĕ-spouz′)
-verb

- Some politicians **espouse** whatever ideas they think will win them votes.
- People who **espouse** animals' rights often find themselves in conflict with scientists who argue for the use of animals in medical experiments.

_a_ *Espouse* means   a. to speak for.   b. to argue against.   c. to study.

3 exhilaration
(ĕg-zǐl′ə-rā′shən)
-noun

- After the last exam of the year, Jan and I were so filled with **exhilaration** that we skipped all the way to the car.
- A marching band gives most people a feeling of **exhilaration**. The lively music makes them feel excited.

_b_ *Exhilaration* means   a. appropriateness.   b. liveliness.   c. commitment.

4 exorbitant
(ĕg-zôr′bǐ-tənt)
-adjective

- Even if I were rich, I wouldn't pay three hundred dollars for those shoes. That's an **exorbitant** price.
- The armed forces often spend **exorbitant** amounts on minor items, including an eight-hundred-dollar ashtray and a toilet seat that cost thousands of dollars.

_c_ *Exorbitant* means   a. estimated.   b. inconvenient.   c. extremely high.

5 extricate
(ĕks′trǐ-kāt′)
-verb

- The fly struggled and struggled but was unable to **extricate** itself from the spider's web.
- The young couple ran up so many debts that they finally needed a counselor to help them **extricate** themselves from their financial mess.

_a_ *Extricate* means   a. to untangle.   b. to distinguish.   c. to excuse.

6 facilitate
(fə-sĭl′ə-tāt′)
-verb

- Automatic doors in supermarkets **facilitate** the entry and exit of customers with bags or shopping carts.
- For those with poor eyesight, large print **facilitates** reading.

_c_ *Facilitate* means   a. to decrease.   b. to cause.   c. to assist.

7 orthodox
(ôr′thə-dŏks′)
-adjective

- When Father McKenzie brought drums and electric guitars into church, he shocked the more **orthodox** members of his congregation.
- The **orthodox** footwear for a sprint or distance race is some kind of running shoes, but a champion Ethiopian runner competed in the Olympics barefoot.

_b_ *Orthodox* means   a. revolutionary.   b. traditional.   c. important.

8 rejuvenate
(rĭ-jōō′və-nāt′)
-verb

- The Fountain of Youth was a legendary spring whose water could **rejuvenate** people.
- The grass had become brown and matted, but a warm spring rain **rejuvenated** it, perking it up and turning it green again.

_c_ *Rejuvenate* means   a. to set free.   b. to excite.   c. to give new life to.

9 synchronize
(sĭng′krə-nīz′)
-verb

- The secret agents **synchronized** their watches so that they could cross the border at exactly the same minute.
- We need to **synchronize** the clocks in our house: the kitchen clock is ten minutes slower than the alarm clock in the bedroom.

_a_ *Synchronize* means   a. to coordinate.   b. to repair.   c. to find.

10 tenuous
(tĕn′yōō-əs)
-adjective

- It doesn't take much to destroy an already **tenuous** relationship. Something as slight as forgetting to telephone can cause an unstable relationship to collapse.
- Del was opposed to the Equal Rights Amendment, but his position seemed **tenuous**. He couldn't support it with any facts, and his logic was weak.

_a_ *Tenuous* means   a. shaky.   b. easy.   c. established.

Matching Words with Definitions

Following are definitions of the ten words. Clearly write or print each word next to its definition. The sentences above and on the previous page will help you decide on the meaning of each word.

1. _____exhilaration_____   Cheerfulness; high spirits
2. _____extricate_____   To free from a tangled situation or a difficulty
3. _____tenuous_____   Having little substance or basis; weak; poorly supported
4. _____decorum_____   Correctness in behavior and manners; standards or conventions of socially acceptable behavior
5. _____rejuvenate_____   To make (someone) feel or seem young again; to make (something) seem fresh or new again
6. _____espouse_____   To support, argue for, or adopt (an idea or cause)
7. _____synchronize_____   To cause to occur at exactly the same time; to cause (clocks and watches) to agree in time
8. _____facilitate_____   To make easier to do or to get
9. _____orthodox_____   Following established, traditional rules or beliefs, especially in religion; following what is customary or commonly accepted
10. _____exorbitant_____   Excessive, especially in amount, cost, or price; beyond what is reasonable or appropriate

CAUTION: Do not go any further until you are sure the above answers are correct. Then you can use the definitions to help you in the following practices. Your goal is eventually to know the words well enough so that you don't need to check the definitions at all.

➤ *Sentence Check 1*

Using the answer line provided, complete each item below with the correct word from the box. Use each word once.

a. **decorum**	b. **espouse**	c. **exhilaration**	d. **exorbitant**	e. **extricate**
f. **facilitate**	g. **orthodox**	h. **rejuvenate**	i. **synchronize**	j. **tenuous**

decorum 1. Ignoring all standards of cafeteria ___, students sat on the tables and threw french fries at each other.

tenuous 2. Some premature babies are so tiny and weak that their hold on life is very ___.

rejuvenate 3. The ads for the anti-wrinkle cream claim that it will ___ aging skin.

exorbitant 4. The new restaurant went out of business because of its ___ prices.

exhilaration 5. The children's ___ at the amusement park was contagious—their parents soon felt excited too.

facilitate 6. If you're giving a dinner party, preparing some food platters ahead of time will ___ your work when the guests arrive.

extricate 7. At age two, Patrick got his head stuck between the bars of an iron railing. His parents had to call the fire department to come and ___ him.

espouse 8. During the 1960s and 1970s, there were bitter clashes between those who ___(e)d the United States' involvement in Vietnam and those who were opposed to it.

synchronize 9. New members of the water ballet club have trouble coordinating their swimming, but with practice, the group is able to ___ its movements.

orthodox 10. "The ___ treatment in this kind of case," the doctor said, "is surgery followed by chemotherapy. But some specialists are exploring the possibility of using surgery alone."

NOTE: Now check your answers to these questions by turning to page 130. Going over the answers carefully will help you prepare for the next two practices, for which answers are not given.

➤ *Sentence Check 2*

Using the answer lines provided, complete each item below with **two** words from the box. Use each word once.

exhilaration
synchronize 1–2. It filled the audience with ___ to see the dancers in the chorus line ___ their turns and kicks so perfectly.

orthodox
tenuous 3–4. In any religion, ___ practices are slow to change. New ones are always in a(n) ___ position at first and require time to become widely accepted.

exorbitant
rejuvenate 5–6. Although it seems ___, an expensive vacation may be worth the money, as it can often ___ one's mind and body.

_____ *decorum* _____   7–8. Foreign Service officers must observe strict rules of conduct. If their
_____ *extricate* _____   behavior violates ___, their government may have to ___ itself from a
                               diplomatic mess.

_____ *espouse* _____   9–10. My grandmother ___(e)d garlic as a treatment for chest colds, in the
_____ *facilitate* _____   belief that it ___(e)d breathing. Sometimes she made us eat it, and
                               sometimes she rubbed it on our chests. As a result, our friends, who
                               found the smell of garlic repugnant°, often refused to be with us.

➤ *Final Check:* Twelve Grown Men in a Bug

Here is a final opportunity for you to strengthen your knowledge of the ten words. First read the following
selection carefully. Then fill in each blank with a word from the box at the top of the previous page.
(Context clues will help you figure out which word goes in which blank.) Use each word once.

My college reunions are very traditional occasions, but there is usually very little that's

(1)_____ *orthodox* _____ about my husband's.

Take, for example, one of the final events of his reunion last year. It all began when a big,
bearded man stood up to address the noisy campus crowd. The man yelled, "You are about to see
an amazing sight. The twelve large, robust° hunks of manhood you see up here, none with a
waistline smaller than forty-two inches, are about to squeeze into this Volkswagen Beetle. We're

not here to (2)_____ *espouse* _____ the use of economy cars, and we're not masochists° trying
to torture ourselves. It's just that we all fit into the Beetle twenty years ago, and we aim to do it

again today. Unless we occasionally (3)_____ *rejuvenate* _____ ourselves by letting go of our
serious side and doing something inane°, how can we stay young?"

"Now, I know that some of you have (4)_____ *exorbitant* _____ bets in the amount of
two whole bucks riding on this," he joked. "We won't fail those who believe in us. And those of

you who consider our claim (5)_____ *tenuous* _____, just watch."

Then the bear of a man turned to the eleven others. "Okay, heroes," he exhorted° them, "this is

no time for (6)_____ *decorum* _____. Forget your manners, and do anything you can to

(7)_____ *facilitate* _____ this mighty task. Now, let's (8)_____ *synchronize* _____ our
start—all together: ready, set, go!"

Shoving, yelling, and cursing, the twelve men tried to squeeze into the car. "If they do get in,"

I said to my husband, "how will they ever (9)_____ *extricate* _____ themselves?"

Moments later, however, everyone was cheering vociferously°. All twelve men were inside the

car. After a few seconds, they exploded out of it, wild with (10)_____ *exhilaration* _____.
Sweaty but triumphant, they jumped up and down and hugged one another.

| *Scores* | Sentence Check 2 _____% | Final Check _____% |

Enter your scores above and in the vocabulary performance chart on the inside back cover of the book.

CHAPTER

15

analogy	placebo
annihilate	proficient
criterion	staunch
emanate	subversive
holistic	vindicate

Ten Words in Context

In the space provided, write the letter of the meaning closest to that of each **boldfaced** word. Use the context of the sentences to help you figure out each word's meaning.

1 analogy
(ə-năl′ə-jē)
-*noun*

- To help students understand vision, teachers often draw an **analogy** between the eye and a camera.
- The commencement address, titled "You Are the Captain of Your Ship," used the **analogy** of life as an ocean-going vessel that the captain must steer between rocks.

_b_ *Analogy* means   a. a picture.   b. a comparison.   c. a standard.

2 annihilate
(ə-nī′ə-lāt′)
-*verb*

- The movie was about a plot to **annihilate** whole cities by poisoning their water supply.
- "Universal Destroyer" is a warlike video game in which the aim is to **annihilate** the opponents.

_c_ *Annihilate* means   a. to escape from.   b. to seize.   c. to wipe out.

3 criterion
(krī-tēr′ē-ən)
-*noun*

- One **criterion** by which writing teachers judge a paper is clear organization.
- Some advertisers aren't concerned about telling the truth. Their only **criterion** for a good commercial is selling the product.

_a_ *Criterion* means   a. a standard.   b. a beginning.   c. an answer.

4 emanate
(ĕm′ə-nāt′)
-*verb*

- As the cinnamon bread baked, a wonderful smell **emanated** from the kitchen.
- The screeching and scraping **emanating** from Keisha's bedroom tell me that she is practicing her violin.

_b_ *Emanate* means   a. to disappear.   b. to come out.   c. to expand.

5 holistic
(hō-lĭs′tĭk)
-*adjective*

- A good drug center takes a **holistic** approach to treatment, seeing each client not just as "an addict" but as a whole person. Along with medical aid, it provides emotional support, individual and family counseling, and follow-up services.
- Eastern cultures tend to take a more **holistic** view of learning than Western societies, focusing on the whole rather than analyzing parts.

_b_ *Holistic* means   a. easygoing.   b. concerned with the whole.   c. nonfinancial.

6 placebo
(plă-sē′bō)
-*noun*

- When the little boy had a headache and there was no aspirin in the house, his mother gave him a **placebo**: a small candy that she told him was a "pain pill." It seemed to work—his headache went away.
- The doctor lost his license when it was found that the "nerve pills" he had been giving to many of his patients were actually a **placebo**—just sugar pills.

_a_ *Placebo* means   a. a fake medication.   b. a natural remedy.   c. an expensive cure.

7 proficient
(prə-fĭsh′ənt)
-*adjective*

- It's not all that hard to become **proficient** on a computer. Be patient, and you'll develop the necessary skill.
- Wayne is a **proficient** woodworker. He is able to make professional-quality desks, bookshelves, and cabinets.

_a_ *Proficient* means   a. highly competent.   b. hard-working.   c. enthusiastic.

8 staunch
(stônch)
-*adjective*

- Although the mayor had been accused of taking bribes, he still had some **staunch** supporters.
- The newspaper's astrological predictions are often way off the mark, yet Tala remains a **staunch** believer in astrology and checks her horoscope every day.

_c_ *Staunch* means   a. busy.   b. unsteady.   c. faithful.

9 subversive
(səb-vûr′sĭv)
-*adjective*

- To some Americans, criticizing the President is a **subversive** act, aimed at undermining his power. To others, it is simply an example of freedom of speech.
- The so-called "consulting company" was a cover for **subversive** activities; it was actually a ring of antigovernment agents.

_b_ *Subversive* means   a. having faith.   b. intended to destroy.   c. blameless.

10 vindicate
(vĭn′də-kāt′)
-*verb*

- When Kai was accused of cheating on a geometry test, he **vindicated** himself by reciting several theorems from memory, proving that he knew the material.
- In our society, people falsely accused of crimes often must spend a great deal of money on legal fees in order to **vindicate** themselves.

_a_ *Vindicate* means   a. to prove innocent.   b. to make a commitment.   c. to weaken.

Matching Words with Definitions

Following are definitions of the ten words. Clearly write or print each word next to its definition. The sentences above and on the previous page will help you decide on the meaning of each word.

1. _____*vindicate*_____   To clear from blame or suspicion; justify or prove right

2. _____*placebo*_____   A substance which contains no medicine, but which the receiver believes is a medicine

3. _____*emanate*_____   To flow or come out from a source; come forth

4. _____*analogy*_____   A comparison between two things in order to clarify or dramatize a point

5. _____*annihilate*_____   To destroy completely; reduce to nothingness

6. _____*criterion*_____   A standard by which something is or can be judged

7. _____*subversive*_____   Acting or intending to undermine or overthrow something established

8. _____*staunch*_____   Firm; loyal; strong in support

9. _____*holistic*_____   Emphasizing the whole and the interdependence of its parts, rather than the parts separately

10. _____*proficient*_____   Skilled; expert

CAUTION: Do not go any further until you are sure the above answers are correct. Then you can use the definitions to help you in the following practices. Your goal is eventually to know the words well enough so that you don't need to check the definitions at all.

➤ *Sentence Check 1*

Using the answer line provided, complete each item below with the correct word from the box. Use each word once.

| a. **analogy** | b. **annihilate** | c. **criterion** | d. **emanate** | e. **holistic** |
| f. **placebo** | g. **proficient** | h. **staunch** | i. **subversive** | j. **vindicate** |

_____subversive_____ 1. During the Vietnam War, some protesters poured blood over draft records. Supporters of the war considered this a ___ act.

_____annihilate_____ 2. Passenger pigeons no longer exist. They were ___(e)d by hunters.

_____staunch_____ 3. I'm a ___ fan of Whitney Houston. I have all her recordings.

_____criterion_____ 4. One ___ used to judge the children's artwork was their use of vivid colors.

_____proficient_____ 5. Although I'm quite a good cook, I'm not very ___ at baking. My pies tend to be runny, and my bread won't rise.

_____holistic_____ 6. A ___ view of business would take into account not just profits but also such things as the work environment and employees' job satisfaction.

_____emanate_____ 7. As the garbage-collectors' strike went into its third week, a dreadful odor began to ___ from all the garbage bags piled up in the city streets.

_____analogy_____ 8. Explaining the importance of using a search engine to find information on the Internet, the instructor used a(n) ___. "The Internet is a huge ocean. The search engine is a guide showing you the best places to fish."

_____vindicate_____ 9. Accused of shoplifting, the customer insisted that she had already paid for the items. She was ___(e)d when she pulled the receipt out of her purse.

_____placebo_____ 10. To test a new painkiller, researchers gave it to one group of volunteers, while a second group got a(n) ___, identical in appearance to the new medicine but with no built-in power to relieve pain.

NOTE: Now check your answers to these questions by turning to page 130. Going over the answers carefully will help you prepare for the next two practices, for which answers are not given.

➤ *Sentence Check 2*

Using the answer lines provided, complete each item below with **two** words from the box. Use each word once.

_____emanate_____
_____annihilate_____ 1–2. From the nasty smell that ___(e)d from the kitchen, I guessed that Mom was using a new kind of bug spray to try to ___ the ants there.

_____criterion_____
_____proficient_____ 3–4. "One ___ by which I'll judge your papers," the teacher said, "is whether you are ___ at connecting your ideas into a cohesive° whole."

_____vindicate_____
_____subversive_____ 5–6. The agent was accused of selling government secrets, but he was able to ___ himself by proving that it was his boss who was the ___ one.

_____ *holistic* _____   7–8. To explain why she supported ___ medicine, the doctor used a(n) ___.
_____ *analogy* _____   She said that taking a narrow view of a health problem is like treating a
                             dying tree's leaves but ignoring its roots, where the real problem lies.

_____ *staunch* _____   9–10. Anton is a(n) ___ believer in the power of a ___. When his small
_____ *placebo* _____   daughter started having nightmares about monsters, he sprayed the
                             room with water and told her it was "anti-monster medicine."

➤ *Final Check:* A Different Kind of Doctor

Here is a final opportunity for you to strengthen your knowledge of the ten words. First read the following selection carefully. Then fill in each blank with a word from the box at the top of the previous page. (Context clues will help you figure out which word goes in which blank.) Use each word once.

Dr. Wilson considers (1)_____ *holistic* _____ medicine the optimum° approach to health care. He believes that to facilitate° healing and well-being, it is imperative° to consider a patient's entire lifestyle, not just specific aches and pains. To explain to patients how to keep well, he uses the (2)_____ *analogy* _____ of a garden. "If a garden gets too much or too little rain, sun, or fertilizer, it won't do well," he says. "But a proper balance keeps the body healthy. In the same way, the body needs proper amounts of good food, exercise, work, and relaxation."

Dr. Wilson often treats patients without giving them drugs. Many of his patients have begun to feel healthier since they started taking his advice. They've adopted such new habits as eating more vegetables and taking a brisk walk every day. As a result, a new liveliness and an increased sense of pleasure and exhilaration° seem to (3)_____ *emanate* _____ from them; many say they feel rejuvenated°.

Despite Dr. Wilson's successes, many orthodox° physicians do not sanction° his methods, and some even deplore° them. They see him as dangerously (4)_____ *subversive* _____, a threat to the medical establishment, and they scoff° at his drug-free "prescriptions," calling them powerless (5)_____ *placebo* _____s. They fear he wants to (6)_____ *annihilate* _____ medical progress.

Dr. Wilson, however, has no wish to destroy medical progress. To the contrary, he believes that his methods represent such progress and that they are (7)_____ *vindicate* _____(e)d by the improved health of his patients. There are other doctors worldwide who agree and who believe he is so (8)_____ *proficient* _____ at medicine that they often invite him to speak at professional conferences.

Dr. Wilson's patients also believe he is highly skilled, and they are the ones who are his most (9)_____ *staunch* _____ supporters. They judge him by a different (10)_____ *criterion* _____ from those who think medical progress lies only in finding new ways to treat disease. They judge him by the extent to which he helps his patients stay well.

Scores Sentence Check 2 _____%	Final Check _____%

Enter your scores above and in the vocabulary performance chart on the inside back cover of the book.

UNIT THREE: *Review*

The box at the right lists twenty-five words from Unit Three. Using the clues at the bottom of the page, fill in these words to complete the puzzle that follows.

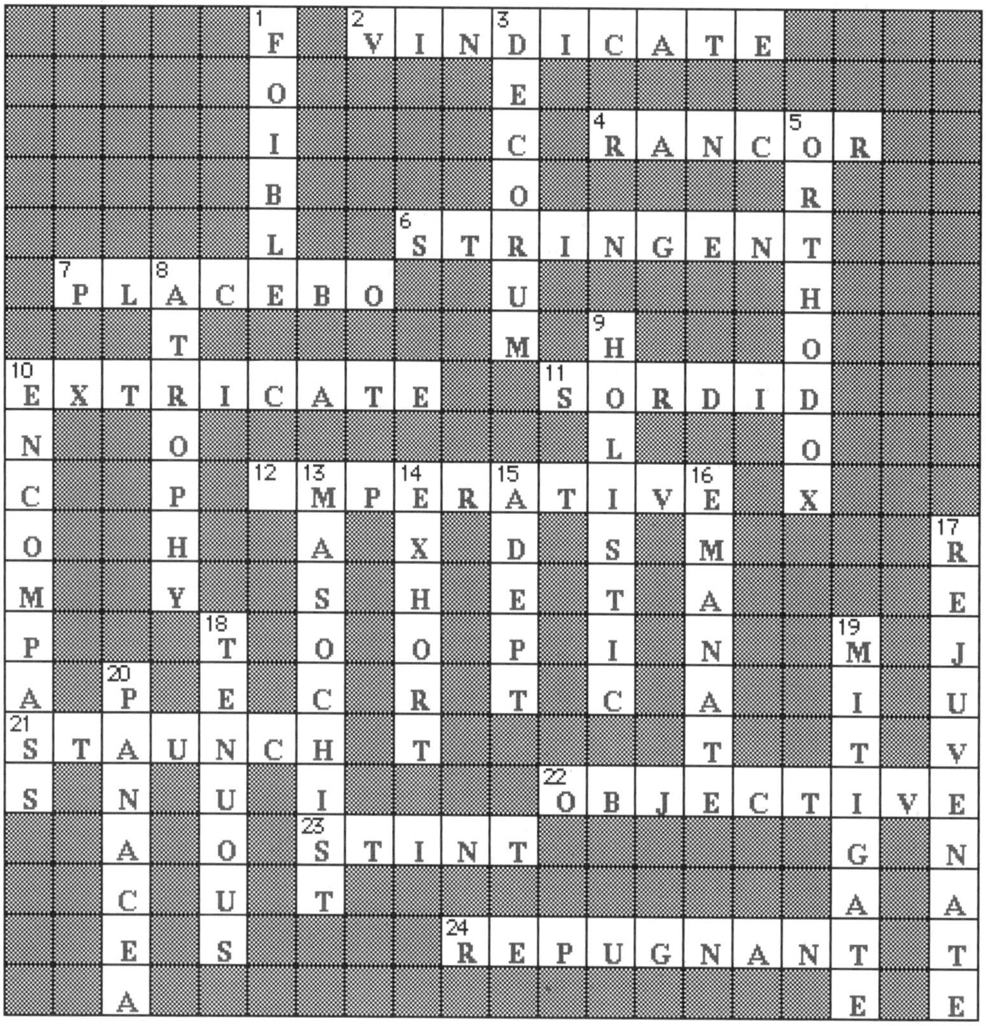

The crossword grid contains the following filled answers:

- 2 Across / 1,2,3 Down area: F, V I N D I C A T E
- 4 Across: R A N C O R
- 6 Across: S T R I N G E N T
- 7 Across: P L A C E B O
- 10 Across: E X T R I C A T E
- 11 Across: S O R D I D
- 12 Across: I M P E R A T I V E
- 21 Across: S T A U N C H
- 22 Across: O B J E C T I V E
- 23 Across: S T I N T
- 24 Across: R E P U G N A N T

Word list box:

adept
atrophy
decorum
emanate
encompass
exhort
extricate
foible
holistic
imperative
masochist
mitigate
objective
orthodox
panacea
placebo
rancor
rejuvenate
repugnant
sordid
staunch
stint
stringent
tenuous
vindicate

ACROSS

2. To clear from blame or suspicion; prove right
4. Intense hatred or resentment
6. Strictly controlled or enforced; strict; severe
7. A substance which contains no medicine, which the receiver believes is medicine
10. To free from a tangled situation or a difficulty
11. Indecent; corrupt
12. Necessary; urgent
21. Firm; loyal; strong in support
22. Not influenced by emotion or personal prejudice
23. A period of work or service
24. Offensive; repulsive

DOWN

1. A minor weakness or character flaw
3. Correctness in behavior and manners
5. Following established, traditional rules or beliefs, especially in religion
8. To wear down, lose strength, or become weak
9. Emphasizing the whole and the interdependence of its parts
10. To include; contain
13. A person who gains satisfaction from suffering pain
14. To urge with argument or strong advice; plead earnestly
15. Highly skilled; expert
16. To flow or come out from a source; come forth
17. To make (someone) feel or seem young again
18. Having little substance or basis; weak; poorly supported
19. To make less severe or less intense; relieve
20. Something supposed to cure all diseases or evils

UNIT THREE: Test 1

PART A
Choose the word that best completes each item and write it in the space provided.

stint   1. My ___ as a worker in the hotel laundry lasted only a day. It turned out that I was allergic to the soap.

    a. placebo   b. analogy   c. foible   d. stint

sordid   2. Working-class housing in nineteenth-century England was ___ by today's standards: crowded, dark, badly ventilated, and unsanitary.

    a. innocuous   b. meticulous   c. sordid   d. holistic

standardized   3. Even when textbooks are ___ throughout a school system, methods of teaching may vary greatly.

    a. standardized   b. emanated   c. vindicated   d. eradicated

exhilaration   4. Hang-gliding produces a feeling of ___ that few other activities can match.

    a. exhilaration   b. decorum   c. criterion   d. atrophy

emanates   5. Superstitious people believe that a cold, clammy wind ___ from the "haunted" house on Elm Street.

    a. synchronizes   b. vindicates   c. emanates   d. mitigates

synchronize   6. To ___ their movements so well, the dancers must practice doing the steps together for hours.

    a. deplore   b. extricate   c. mitigate   d. synchronize

decorum   7. Rules of ___ change over the years. For instance, my grandmother says that a lady always wears a hat to church, but few young women do so nowadays.

    a. analogy   b. decorum   c. panacea   d. placebo

subversive   8. In order to find a ring of spies trying to learn military secrets, the government agent pretended to be involved in ___ activities.

    a. staunch   b. tenuous   c. holistic   d. subversive

annihilate   9. It's amazing how I can ___ a thousand mosquitoes with bug spray, and an hour later another thousand appear.

    a. espouse   b. annihilate   c. facilitate   d. vindicate

entrepreneur   10. Years ago, a shrewd ___ got the idea of selling "pet rocks" and made a fortune when they became a fad.

    a. criterion   b. analogy   c. placebo   d. entrepreneur

(Continues on next page)

PART B

On the answer line, write the letter of the choice that best completes each item.

___b___ 11. My mother considered baked custard a **panacea**. According to her, it
    a. was the worst-tasting thing in the world.   b. cured anything from flu to a broken heart.
    c. should be saved for special occasions.   d. tasted good, but was not good for us.

___d___ 12. A truly **unprecedented** event would be
    a. an eclipse of the sun.   b. a musical as good as *West Side Story*.
    c. the landing of humans on the moon.   d. a TV interview with an alien life form.

___a___ 13. Right after his heart attack, Alec's grip on life was so **tenuous** that his doctors
    a. did not expect him to live.   b. admired his fighting spirit.
    c. were amazed at his quick recovery.   d. realized the heart attack had been mild.

___a___ 14. When my boyfriend of two years dumped me, I wasn't surprised to hear my **staunch** friend say,
    a. "He wasn't good enough for you, anyway."   b. "I don't want to hear about it."
    c. "Would you mind if I started dating him?"   d. "It was probably your fault."

___d___ 15. Rita wears **flamboyant** hairstyles. Today, her hair is
    a. chin-length.   b. in a ponytail.
    c. easily cared for.   d. in green braids.

___d___ 16. When Annabelle broke off their engagement, Arthur showed he was **magnanimous** by saying,
    a. "How weird. I was just about to dump *you*."   b. "You don't deserve me, and that's that."
    c. "I'm the unhappiest man in the world."   d. "*Please* keep the three-carat diamond ring."

___d___ 17. When told he needed to have an operation, the **masochist**
    a. panicked, saying, "I just can't face that."   b. wanted a second opinion.
    c. assumed that he would die.   d. secretly hoped it would hurt quite a lot.

___c___ 18. It was **presumptuous** of my brother to
    a. volunteer his free time to work at a homeless shelter.
    b. refuse to lend money to his spendthrift pal Leon.
    c. call elderly, dignified Mr. Jackson "Larry" as soon as he met him.
    d. start giggling in the middle of a quiet church service.

___c___ 19. Commenting on the **exorbitant** prices in the restaurant, Willy said,
    a. "No wonder the restaurant is popular—it's such a bargain!"
    b. "The prices don't make sense—why is the lobster less expensive than the spaghetti?"
    c. "A cup of soup here costs more than a full meal anywhere else!"
    d. "Nothing is cheap, but nothing is very expensive either—the prices are reasonable."

___b___ 20. Because Ben and Susan had asked for **utilitarian** wedding gifts, a group of friends bought them
    a. whoopee cushions, rubber chickens, and fake spiders dangling from long threads.
    b. a set of dishes and silverware.
    c. silk bedsheets, French champagne, and Russian caviar.
    d. dozens of roses to decorate their apartment.

Score   (Number correct) _____ x 4 = _____ %

Enter your score above and in the vocabulary performance chart on the inside back cover of the book.

UNIT THREE: Test 2

PART A
Complete each item with a word from the box. Use each word once.

a. **atrophy**	b. **criterion**	c. **deplore**	d. **deprivation**	e. **eradicate**
f. **exhort**	g. **extricate**	h. **foible**	i. **objective**	j. **placebo**
k. **recrimination**	l. **rejuvenate**	m. **repugnant**		

repugnant 1. The furry white and green mold growing on the old tomato sauce was a(n) ___ sight.

foible 2. One of my ___s is biting into many chocolates in a box until I find one I like.

eradicate 3. If the common cold were ever ___(e)d, it would be economically unhealthy for the makers of cold remedies.

exhort 4. The TV preacher ___(e)d viewers to support his ministry with whatever funds they could manage to send.

objective 5. Judging people by their appearance makes it difficult to be ___ about their personalities.

criterion 6. One ___ I use in selecting clothing is that an item be made out of a comfortable fabric.

deprivation 7. After Chrissy stayed awake studying for seventy-two hours, sleep ___ caused her to start having double vision and to hear voices that weren't there.

extricate 8. The little boy's foot was so firmly caught in the folding chair that it took three adults to ___ him.

rejuvenate 9. My mother was feeling twice her age before her trip to Arizona, but the relaxing vacation really ___(e)d her.

deplore 10. Although I ___ the conditions that face children born to drug addicts, I don't know what to do to help.

atrophy 11. The day after surgery, the nurses got Alonso out of bed and walking, so that his muscles would not begin to ___.

recrimination 12. The two brothers will never make peace until they stop reacting to every accusation with another accusation. Such ___s only lead to more arguing.

placebo 13. When little Sarah couldn't sleep, her mother gave her a ___ and called it a "magic sleeping potion." It was a glass of milk tinted red with food coloring.

(Continues on next page)

PART B
Write **C** if the italicized word is used **correctly**. Write **I** if the word is used **incorrectly**.

_C_ 14. In an *orthodox* classroom, students' desks are lined up in rows.

_C_ 15. Only female black widow spiders are dangerous to humans. The bite of a male is *innocuous*.

_I_ 16. The load of oil dumped on the highway *facilitated* the flow of traffic for more than three hours.

_I_ 17. I didn't know that Jerry was so *proficient* in geography until I saw that F on his report card.

_I_ 18. Ricardo writes thoughtful essays and then spoils them by handing in a *meticulous* final draft filled with spelling and typing errors.

_C_ 19. It is *imperative* that my mother get her cholesterol level down, as she is now at high risk of a heart attack.

_I_ 20. Lily's ankle injury is severe, but the doctor told her a couple of days of bed rest will *exacerbate* the sprain enough so that she can walk again.

_C_ 21. Lois and Manny were divorced three years ago, and they still feel such *rancor* that they refuse to speak to each other.

_I_ 22. It was bad enough being grounded, but my father is going to *mitigate* my punishment by stopping my allowance.

_C_ 23. The defendant, accused of murder, proclaimed his innocence and was *vindicated* when a man who looked just like him confessed.

_I_ 24. As kids, my brother and I loved staying with our grandparents because of their *stringent* rules; they let us stay up as late as we liked and eat candy for breakfast.

_C_ 25. The nursery school teacher used the *analogy* of a flower garden to describe her class, saying that just as each flower has its own special beauty, so does each child.

> *Score*   (Number correct) _____ x 4 = _____ %

Enter your score above and in the vocabulary performance chart on the inside back cover of the book.

UNIT THREE: Test 3

PART A: Synonyms

In the space provided, write the letter of the choice that is most nearly the **same** in meaning as the **boldfaced** word.

  _a_   1. **synchronize**   a) make happen together   b) ease   c) weaken   d) urge

  _b_   2. **objective**   a) bold   b) based on facts   c) shy   d) based on emotions

  _c_   3. **stint**   a) standard   b) lack   c) work period   d) businessperson

  _b_   4. **analogy**   a) skill   b) comparison   c) lesson   d) sermon

  _c_   5. **imperative**   a) helpful   b) beautiful   c) essential   d) reasonable

  _a_   6. **foible**   a) imperfection   b) goal   c) personality characteristic   d) skill

  _c_   7. **entrepreneur**   a) politician   b) boss   c) business organizer and investor   d) leader

  _b_   8. **decorum**   a) blame   b) correctness in manners   c) flaw   d) decoration

  _d_   9. **deprivation**   a) dislike   b) discipline   c) necessity   d) lack

  _a_   10. **holistic**   a) all-inclusive   b) partial   c) healthy   d) skillful

  _c_   11. **criterion**   a) emotion   b) insult   c) standard   d) habit

  _a_   12. **exhort**   a) urge   b) criticize   c) agree   d) oppose

  _b_   13. **emanate**   a) delay   b) come forth   c) stay   d) destroy

  _a_   14. **proficient**   a) skilled   b) innocent   c) rebellious   d) immoral

  _d_   15. **masochist**   a) messy person   b) servant   c) actor   d) one who welcomes pain

  _a_   16. **subversive**   a) intended to overthrow   b) supportive   c) distasteful   d) beneath

  _c_   17. **eradicate**   a) blame   b) break   c) destroy   d) dislike

  _d_   18. **extricate**   a) advise   b) make joyful   c) rebel   d) rescue

  _b_   19. **mitigate**   a) ignore   b) ease   c) change   d) worsen

  _b_   20. **presumptuous**   a) unskilled   b) bold   c) timid   d) skilled

  _c_   21. **standardize**   a) destroy   b) prove innocent   c) make the same   d) make worse

  _a_   22. **recrimination**   a) countercharge   b) just punishment   c) second thoughts   d) sadness

  _d_   23. **panacea**   a) epidemic   b) ill will   c) support   d) cure-all

  _c_   24. **utilitarian**   a) showy   b) spoken   c) practical   d) urgent

  _c_   25. **placebo**   a) universal remedy   b) peacefulness   c) make-believe medicine   d) disease

(Continues on next page)

PART B: Antonyms
In the space provided, write the letter of the choice that is most nearly the **opposite** in meaning to the **boldfaced** word.

_d_ 26. **unprecedented**   a) helpful   b) moral   c) strong   d) common

_b_ 27. **vindicate**   a) look back   b) blame   c) look forward   d) help

_a_ 28. **atrophy**   a) strengthen   b) win   c) support   d) claim

_b_ 29. **meticulous**   a) broken   b) careless   c) temporary   d) unpopular

_c_ 30. **deplore**   a) question   b) provide   c) approve of   d) know of

_c_ 31. **exorbitant**   a) legal   b) high   c) inexpensive   d) happy

_b_ 32. **adept**   a) unknown   b) unskilled   c) unpleasant   d) unforgiving

_d_ 33. **magnanimous**   a) physically small   b) inexpensive   c) perfect   d) unforgiving

_a_ 34. **encompass**   a) exclude   b) get lost   c) prevent   d) do one at a time

_c_ 35. **exhilaration**   a) weakness   b) immorality   c) sadness   d) coming in

_a_ 36. **facilitate**   a) make more difficult   b) face   c) disapprove of   d) make older

_d_ 37. **sordid**   a) talented   b) colorful   c) peaceful   d) honorable

_c_ 38. **annihilate**   a) approve of   b) beautify   c) create   d) welcome

_a_ 39. **espouse**   a) oppose   b) participate   c) ignore   d) misrepresent

_b_ 40. **rancor**   a) good manners   b) goodwill   c) good looks   d) good luck

_c_ 41. **innocuous**   a) all-inclusive   b) too expensive   c) harmful   d) distasteful

_d_ 42. **exacerbate**   a) come forth   b) agree   c) build   d) improve

_a_ 43. **repugnant**   a) pleasant   b) wise   c) important   d) loyal

_b_ 44. **stringent**   a) incorrect   b) flexible   c) caring   d) usual

_c_ 45. **rejuvenate**   a) disappoint   b) blame   c) make older   d) cause to agree in time

_a_ 46. **homogeneous**   a) varied   b) similar   c) wild   d) ignorant

_c_ 47. **flamboyant**   a) explosive   b) cool   c) dull   d) cheap

_a_ 48. **orthodox**   a) untraditional   b) not required   c) generous   d) impractical

_c_ 49. **tenuous**   a) relaxed   b) reversed   c) well supported   d) partial

_b_ 50. **staunch**   a) small   b) unfaithful   c) boring   d) rich

Score   (Number correct) _____ x 2 = _____%

Enter your score above and in the vocabulary performance chart on the inside back cover of the book.

UNIT THREE: Test 4

Each item below starts with a pair of words in CAPITAL LETTERS. For each item, figure out the relationship between these two words. Then decide which of the choices (*a*, *b*, *c*, or *d*) expresses a similar relationship. Write the letter of your choice on the answer line.

_c_ 1. ADEPT : PICKPOCKET ::

    a. thin : chess player   b. scholarly : shortstop
    c. graceful : dancer   d. cheerful : worrier

_d_ 2. ENCOMPASS : EXCLUDE ::

    a. explain : clarify   b. insert : write
    c. erase : remove   d. omit : include

_b_ 3. ENTREPRENEUR : BUSINESS ::

    a. dentist : patient   b. producer : movie
    c. cook : fry   d. company : employee

_c_ 4. HOMOGENEOUS : MILK ::

    a. juicy : cornflakes   b. fattening : celery
    c. grainy : sugar   d. greasy : water

_a_ 5. FLAMBOYANT : GRAY SUIT ::

    a. economical : ten-course banquet   b. generous : thirty-percent tip
    c. luxurious : palace   d. competitive : Olympics

_b_ 6. FOIBLE : NAIL-BITING ::

    a. weakness : self-control   b. phobia : fear of heights
    c. strength : compulsive gambling   d. skill : blue eyes

_d_ 7. MAGNANIMOUS : GENEROUS ::

    a. angelic : heaven   b. softhearted : brutal
    c. delicate : flower   d. affectionate : loving

_c_ 8. REPUGNANT : COCKROACHES ::

    a. cheerful : ants   b. sturdy : butterflies
    c. welcome : songbirds   d. ruthless : doves

_d_ 9. DEPLORE : SIN ::

    a. praise : crime   b. foretell : predict
    c. forget : forgiveness   d. seek : wisdom

_c_ 10. OBJECTIVE : JUDGE ::

    a. treacherous : jury   b. sluggish : rock group
    c. knowledgeable : teacher   d. obedient : parent

(Continues on next page)

_c_ 11. UTILITARIAN : FRYING PAN ::

    a. useless : doorway   b. electrical : water pipes

    c. decorative : wallpaper   d. portable : foundation

_b_ 12. UNPRECEDENTED : FAMILIAR ::

    a. injurious : accidental   b. horrible : pleasant

    c. abundant : plentiful   d. questioning : curious

_d_ 13. EXHILARATION : WALKING ON AIR ::

    a. anxiety: being cool as a cucumber   b. weariness : being fresh as a daisy

    c. ambitious : drifting along   d. depression : being down in the dumps

_c_ 14. ESPOUSE : DENOUNCE ::

    a. dislike : enemies   b. study : learn

    c. complain : praise   d. distrust : doubt

_a_ 15. FACILITATE : MAKE EASIER ::

    a. postpone : delay   b. speak : speech

    c. exaggerate : understate   d. fence : post

_c_ 16. EXTRICATE : FREE ::

    a. read : write   b. add : subtract

    c. pledge : promise   d. ignore : celebrate

_b_ 17. ANALOGY : COMPARISON ::

    a. anatomy : music   b. anthology : collection

    c. astronomy : medicine   d. anonymity : fame

_c_ 18. HOLISTIC : WHOLE ::

    a. skeptical : positive   b. physical : mental

    c. fragmentary : part   d. weekly : monthly

_d_ 19. PLACEBO : SUGAR PILL ::

    a. health : vitamins   b. prescription : subscription

    c. leaf : lettuce   d. dwelling : igloo

_b_ 20. PROFICIENT : INCAPABLE ::

    a. talented : artistic   b. fake : genuine

    c. immaculate : reputation   d. perceptive : observer

Score   (Number correct) _____ x 5 = _____ %

Enter your score above and in the vocabulary performance chart on the inside back cover of the book.

Unit Four

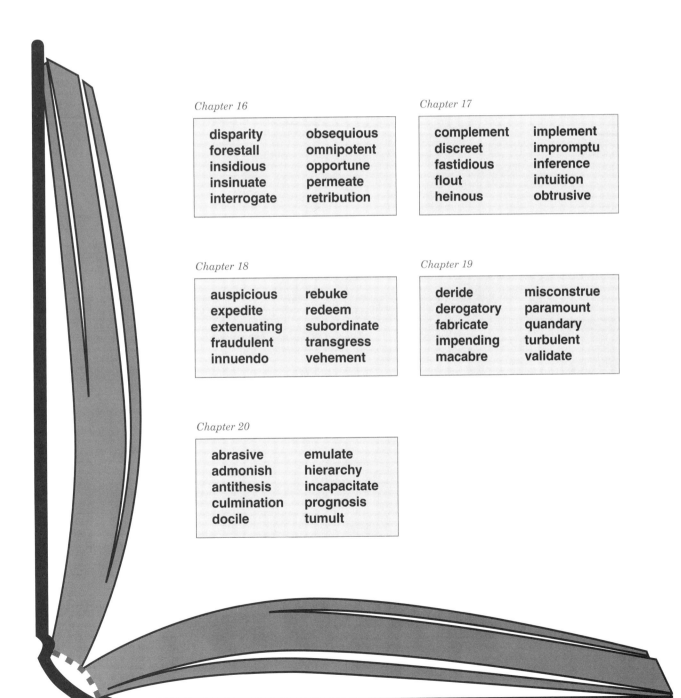

Chapter 16

disparity	obsequious
forestall	omnipotent
insidious	opportune
insinuate	permeate
interrogate	retribution

Chapter 17

complement	implement
discreet	impromptu
fastidious	inference
flout	intuition
heinous	obtrusive

Chapter 18

auspicious	rebuke
expedite	redeem
extenuating	subordinate
fraudulent	transgress
innuendo	vehement

Chapter 19

deride	misconstrue
derogatory	paramount
fabricate	quandary
impending	turbulent
macabre	validate

Chapter 20

abrasive	emulate
admonish	hierarchy
antithesis	incapacitate
culmination	prognosis
docile	tumult

CHAPTER

16

disparity	obsequious
forestall	omnipotent
insidious	opportune
insinuate	permeate
interrogate	retribution

Ten Words in Context

In the space provided, write the letter of the meaning closest to that of each **boldfaced** word. Use the context of the sentences to help you figure out each word's meaning.

1 **disparity**
(dĭ-spăr′ə-tē)
-noun

- There's an enormous **disparity** between the million-dollar incomes of top executives and the modest paychecks most people earn.
- Shirley and Jason don't let the **disparity** in their ages weaken their marriage, but Jason's mother isn't happy with a daughter-in-law her own age.

_b_ *Disparity* means   a. a combination.   b. a gap.   c. a closeness.

2 **forestall**
(fôr-stôl′)
-verb

- The owners of the failing store hoped that the huge sale would bring in enough cash to **forestall** bankruptcy.
- When the environmentalists were unable to **forestall** the destruction of the forest by legal means, they lay down in front of the developer's bulldozers.

_a_ *Forestall* means   a. to keep from happening.   b. to predict.   c. to pay for.

3 **insidious**
(ĭn-sĭd′ē-əs)
-adjective

- Lyme disease is **insidious** because although it is very serious, it starts with a nearly invisible tick bite, and its early symptoms are mild.
- Many people fear that farm chemicals have **insidious** effects. The chemicals don't seem harmful, but cancer rates have started to increase.

_b_ *Insidious* means   a. badly timed.   b. subtly harmful.   c. all-powerful.

4 **insinuate**
(ĭn-sĭn′yōō-āt′)
-verb

- He didn't come right out and say it, but Mr. Shriber **insinuated** that someone in the class had gotten hold of the test ahead of time.
- "You always find time to help Sandy with her homework," my sister said to me, as if to **insinuate** that I was flirting with Sandy.

_a_ *Insinuate* means   a. to hint.   b. to wish.   c. to state directly.

5 **interrogate**
(ĭn-tĕr′ə-gāt′)
-verb

- Before the police **interrogated** the suspect, they informed him of his right not to answer their questions.
- "You never just ask me if I had a nice time with my date," Leonard complained to his parents. "Instead, you sit me down at the kitchen table and **interrogate** me."

_a_ *Interrogate* means   a. to ask questions.   b. to delay.   c. to abuse.

6 **obsequious**
(ŏb-sē′kwē-əs)
-adjective

- Each of the queen's advisers tried to be more **obsequious** than the other, bowing as low as possible and uttering flowery compliments.
- Marge constantly flatters the boss, calls him "sir," and agrees loudly with everything he says. However, her **obsequious** behavior only annoys him.

_b_ *Obsequious* means   a. unequal in rank.   b. overly eager to please.   c. methodical.

7 omnipotent
(ŏm-nĭp′ə-tənt)
-adjective

- Small children think of their parents as **omnipotent**—able to do anything, control everything, and grant whatever a child might wish for.
- The American government is designed so that no one branch can be **omnipotent**. Congress, the President, and the Supreme Court share power and hold each other in check.

_c_ *Omnipotent* means   a. totally good.   b. willing to serve.   c. all-powerful.

8 opportune
(ŏp′ər-tōon′)
-adjective

- Renee thought that her parents' anniversary would be an **opportune** time to announce her own engagement. They could have a double celebration.
- The job offer came at an especially **opportune** time. I had just decided that I might like to work for a year or so before returning to school.

_a_ *Opportune* means   a. appropriate.   b. difficult.   c. early.

9 permeate
(pûr′mē-āt′)
-verb

- The strong scent of Kate's perfume soon **permeated** the entire room.
- The weather was so rainy and damp that moisture seemed to **permeate** everything: curtains hung limp, towels wouldn't dry, and windows were fogged over.

_b_ *Permeate* means   a. to harm.   b. to penetrate.   c. to make unclear.

10 retribution
(rĕ′trə-byōo′shən)
-noun

- Some "sins" in life have their own built-in **retribution**. For example, if you get drunk, you'll have a hangover; if you overeat, you'll gain weight.
- For much of human history, before science could explain diseases, many people believed that any illness was a **retribution** for immoral behavior.

_c_ *Retribution* means   a. an inequality.   b. an obstacle.   c. a penalty.

Matching Words with Definitions

Following are definitions of the ten words. Clearly write or print each word next to its definition. The sentences above and on the previous page will help you decide on the meaning of each word.

1. _____obsequious_____ Overly willing to serve, obey, or flatter in order to gain favor
2. _____insinuate_____ To suggest slyly
3. _____retribution_____ Something given or done as repayment, reward, or (usually) punishment
4. _____disparity_____ An inequality or difference, as in ages or amounts
5. _____insidious_____ Working or spreading harmfully but in a manner hard to notice; more harmful than at first is evident
6. _____permeate_____ To flow or spread throughout (something)
7. _____opportune_____ Suitable (said of time); well-timed
8. _____forestall_____ To prevent or hinder by taking action beforehand
9. _____omnipotent_____ All-powerful; having unlimited power or authority
10. _____interrogate_____ To question formally and systematically

CAUTION: Do not go any further until you are sure the above answers are correct. Then you can use the definitions to help you in the following practices. Your goal is eventually to know the words well enough so that you don't need to check the definitions at all.

➤ *Sentence Check 1*

Using the answer line provided, complete each item below with the correct word from the box. Use each word once.

a. disparity	b. forestall	c. insidious	d. insinuate	e. interrogate
f. obsequious	g. omnipotent	h. opportune	i. permeate	j. retribution

permeate   1. When our dog was sprayed by a skunk, the smell soon ___(e)d the house.

forestall   2. To ___ complaints about unrepaired potholes, the township set up a "pothole hotline" and promised to fill in any reported hole within two days.

opportune   3. Because no one else's hand was raised, I considered it a(n) ___ moment to ask a question.

interrogate   4. In many countries, political prisoners who are being ___(e)d by the secret police are likely to be tortured in an attempt to force answers from them.

retribution   5. When the Earl of Essex plotted against his queen, Elizabeth I of England, ___ was swift and harsh: she had him beheaded for treason.

disparity   6. "There seems to be quite a ___," Shannon objected to the car dealer, "between your cost and the sticker price."

insidious   7. The effects of certain prescription drugs, such as Valium, can be ___. People who take them may slip into addiction without being aware of it.

omnipotent   8. According to legend, King Canute—an ancient ruler of England, Denmark, and Norway—thought he was ___. He actually ordered the tide to stop rising.

insinuate   9. Instead of directly saying "Buy our product," many ads use slick images to ___ that the product will give the buyer sex appeal, power, or prestige.

obsequious   10. The headwaiter's manner toward customers who looked rich was ___. Ignoring the rest of us, he gave them the restaurant's best tables and hovered over them, all smiles.

NOTE: Now check your answers to these questions by turning to page 130. Going over the answers carefully will help you prepare for the next two practices, for which answers are not given.

➤ *Sentence Check 2*

Using the answer lines provided, complete each item below with **two** words from the box. Use each word once.

disparity
insinuate   1–2. The wide ___ between men's and women's pay in the company led to a protest by the women. The management tried to squelch° the protest and ___(e)d that the women were subversive° and were trying to ruin company morale.

insidious
permeate   3–4. The chemical spray used to eradicate° tentworms had ___ effects: after killing the worms, it gradually seeped down, ___(e)d the soil, and poisoned Duck Lake.

_____ *retribution* _____ 5–6. The ex-convict was filled with rancor°. As ___ for his years in prison, he planned to attack, at the first ___ moment, the judge who had sentenced him.

_____ *opportune* _____

_____ *omnipotent* _____ 7–8. The remote control of my VCR makes me feel ___. I can ___ any disaster—a fire, a flood, an earthquake, a sordid° crime—by pressing a button and stopping the movie dead.

_____ *forestall* _____

_____ *interrogate* _____ 9–10. In a job interview, use discretion°. Don't react as though you were being ___(e)d by the police; but don't be ___ either, as if the interviewer were a king or queen and you were a humble servant.

_____ *obsequious* _____

➤ *Final Check:* My Devilish Older Sister

Here is a final opportunity for you to strengthen your knowledge of the ten words. First read the following selection carefully. Then fill in each blank with a word from the box at the top of the previous page. (Context clues will help you figure out which word goes in which blank.) Use each word once.

Anyone who thinks older sisters protect younger ones has never heard me tell about my sister Pam. There's no great (1)_____ *disparity* _____ in our ages—Pam is only three years older—but throughout our childhood she was always able to beat me at cards, at jacks, at all board games. This seemingly unlimited power to win made me think of her as (2)_____ *omnipotent* _____. I obeyed all her orders ("Relinquish° that lollipop!") and accepted all her insults ("You're grotesque°!" "You're positively repugnant°!") in the most timid, (3)_____ *obsequious* _____ manner. Privately, I longed for revenge.

When Pam made up her mind to tease or trick me, there was nothing I could do to (4)_____ *forestall* _____ her plans. And she never missed a(n) (5)_____ *opportune* _____ moment to terrorize me. When our old dog growled, for no reason, at the empty air, she would (6)_____ *insinuate* _____ that evil spirits must have (7)_____ *permeate* _____(e)d the atmosphere, saying, "Dogs, you know, can sense the supernatural." Once I made the mistake of revealing that crabs terrified me. After that, I was inundated° with photos of crabs, drawings of crabs, even labels from cans of crabmeat. In retrospect°, though, her worst trick was giving me some "chocolate candy" that I impetuously° gobbled up. It turned out to be Ex-Lax. After that, if Pam offered me anything, no matter how innocuous° it looked, I always (8)_____ *interrogate* _____(e)d her: "What is it really? Do you still have the wrapping? Will you take a bite first?" But this episode also had a more (9)_____ *insidious* _____ effect: for years, I was afraid of new foods.

Now that we're grown, Pam has greatly improved. She no longer likes to torment me, and she even seems contrite° about the past. However, I still sometimes think up various fantasies of (10)_____ *retribution* _____ in which *I* am the older sister, and at last I get my revenge.

Scores Sentence Check 2 _____%	Final Check _____%

Enter your scores above and in the vocabulary performance chart on the inside back cover of the book.

complement	implement
discreet	impromptu
fastidious	inference
flout	intuition
heinous	obtrusive

Ten Words in Context

In the space provided, write the letter of the meaning closest to that of each **boldfaced** word. Use the context of the sentences to help you figure out each word's meaning.

1 complement
(kŏm′plə-mənt)
-verb

- The new singer's voice **complemented** the other voices, rounding out the group's sound.
- A red tie would **complement** Pedro's gray suit and white shirt, giving the outfit a needed touch of color.

_a_ *Complement* means
    a. to go perfectly with.   b. to reach out for.   c. to overpower.

2 discreet
(dĭ-skrēt′)
-adjective

- Once the teacher realized Jared could not read well, she made **discreet** efforts to give him extra help. She didn't want to embarrass him in front of his classmates.
- "Be **discreet** about these drawings, Wilson," the boss said. "Don't show them to just anyone. We don't want another company stealing our designs."

_b_ *Discreet* means
    a. honest.   b. cautious.   c. obvious.

3 fastidious
(făs-tĭd′ē-əs)
-adjective

- Tilly was a **fastidious** housekeeper who vacuumed every day, dusted twice a day, and never allowed so much as a pencil or safety pin to be out of place.
- A **fastidious** dresser, Mr. Lapp never leaves his home without looking as if he has just stepped out of a fashion magazine.

_c_ *Fastidious* means
    a. working quickly.   b. having insight.   c. very particular.

4 flout
(flout)
-verb

- My neighbors were evicted from their apartment because they **flouted** the building's rules. They threw trash in the hallway, had loud all-night parties, and just laughed at anyone who complained.
- The men in the warehouse **flouted** the company's regulations about sexual harassment: they covered the walls with pinups.

_a_ *Flout* means
    a. to mock and defy.   b. to put into effect.   c. to show off.

5 heinous
(hā′nəs)
-adjective

- The decision to drop the atomic bomb on Hiroshima and Nagasaki has been debated for more than half a century: was it a **heinous** crime on the part of the United States, or was it a necessary action to win the war?
- Millions of people were shocked recently by news reports of a **heinous** act: a woman had starved her little daughter to death.

_a_ *Heinous* means
    a. wicked.   b. unplanned.   c. detailed.

6 implement
(ĭm′plə-mĕnt′)
-verb

- NASA expects to **implement** its plan for a mission to Mars in 2015.
- Brett is full of ideas about starting his own business, but he never follows through and **implements** them.

_b_ *Implement* means
    a. to recall.   b. to put into effect.   c. to criticize.

7 **impromptu**
(ĭm-prŏmp'tōō')
-adjective

- My speech at my cousin's birthday dinner was **impromptu**; I hadn't expected to be called on to say anything.
- When Kianna discovered that she and Barry had both brought guitars to the party, she suggested an **impromptu** duet.

_a_ *Impromptu* means   a. not rehearsed.   b. not very good.   c. very quiet.

8 **inference**
(ĭn'fər-əns)
-noun

- Rita said with a wink, "Did you notice how Uncle Joe's hair has miraculously grown back?" My **inference** was that he was wearing a toupee.
- "Where did you buy these pork chops?" asked Harry. "Why? What's wrong with them?" Maria asked, making the **inference** that he didn't like them.

_b_ *Inference* means   a. a statement.   b. a conclusion.   c. a secret.

9 **intuition**
(ĭn'tōō-ĭsh'ən)
-noun

- "I paint by **intuition**," the artist said. "In a flash, I see how a work should look. I don't really think it out."
- "The minute I met your mother," my father said, "my **intuition** told me that we'd get married someday."

_c_ *Intuition* means   a. careful study.   b. memory.   c. instinct.

10 **obtrusive**
(ŏb-trōō'sĭv)
-adjective

- The huge, sprawling new mall seemed **obtrusive** in the quiet little country town.
- My brother's stutter is often hardly noticeable, but when he is nervous or in a hurry, it can become **obtrusive**.

_a_ *Obtrusive* means   a. overly obvious.   b. unplanned.   c. greatly improved.

Matching Words with Definitions

Following are definitions of the ten words. Clearly write or print each word next to its definition. The sentences above and on the previous page will help you decide on the meaning of each word.

1. _____*flout*_____   To treat with scorn or contempt; defy insultingly

2. _____*intuition*_____   The ability to know something without the conscious use of reasoning

3. _____*implement*_____   To carry out; put into practice

4. _____*obtrusive*_____   Undesirably noticeable

5. _____*discreet*_____   Wise in keeping silent about secrets and other information of a delicate nature; prudent; tactful

6. _____*impromptu*_____   Performed or spoken without practice or preparation

7. _____*heinous*_____   Extremely evil; outrageous

8. _____*inference*_____   A conclusion drawn from evidence; an assumption

9. _____*complement*_____   To add (to something or someone) what is lacking or needed; round out; bring to perfection

10. _____*fastidious*_____   Extremely attentive to details; fussy

CAUTION: Do not go any further until you are sure the above answers are correct. Then you can use the definitions to help you in the following practices. Your goal is eventually to know the words well enough so that you don't need to check the definitions at all.

➢ *Sentence Check 1*

Using the answer line provided, complete each item below with the correct word from the box. Use each word once.

a. **complement**	b. **discreet**	c. **fastidious**	d. **flout**	e. **heinous**
f. **implement**	g. **impromptu**	h. **inference**	i. **intuition**	j. **obtrusive**

intuition　　　　1. Rachel's ___ told her not to date a man who kept tropical fish in his bathtub.

flout　　　　2. After Rudy ___(e)d his parents' 11 o'clock curfew—breezing in at 2 a.m. with a cheerful "Hi, folks!"—they took away his car keys for a month.

heinous　　　　3. In the American system of justice, anyone charged with a crime, no matter how ___ the offense, is entitled to be defended by a lawyer.

impromptu　　　　4. The ___ press conference turned out to be a bad idea. The senator should have planned his remarks beforehand.

discreet　　　　5. "Loose lips sink ships" was a famous World War II slogan. It warned Americans to be ___ and not say anything that might reveal military plans.

implement　　　　6. To ___ their plan for a surprise attack on the girls' club, the boys needed squirt guns and a gallon of grape juice.

fastidious　　　　7. The writer Ernest Hemingway had a "tough guy" image but was ___ about using words; he rewrote the ending of one novel forty-four times.

complement　　　　8. Wendy is an excellent hair stylist, because she doesn't just cut hair. She also advises her customers about what hairstyle will ___ their features.

inference　　　　9. Alicia signed her card to Mario "Warm regards." Mario's ___ was that she meant "I feel *only* warm regards, not love."

obtrusive　　　　10. The new partition between the restaurant's smoking and nonsmoking sections looks ___. Some plants or flowers might help it blend in better.

NOTE: Now check your answers to these questions by turning to page 130. Going over the answers carefully will help you prepare for the next two practices, for which answers are not given.

➢ *Sentence Check 2*

Using the answer lines provided, complete each item below with **two** words from the box. Use each word once.

intuition
fastidious　　　　1–2. Although Anne is one of my best friends, my ___ tells me we would not be good roommates. She's so ___ that she irons her bedsheets, while I'm notorious° for cleaning my apartment only once a year.

complement
impromptu　　　　3–4. The dark, rumbling voice of the bass ___(e)d the high, sweet tones of the soprano as they sang a(n) ___ but flawless duet. Having just met, they were surprised and delighted at how good they sounded together.

discreet
inference　　　　5–6. Kay said only, "It would be ___ not to discuss the missing funds in front of Debra." But she meant us to make this ___: "I think she stole them."

_____ implement _____   7–8. Connoisseurs° of science fiction love one movie in which evil alien
_____ heinous _____   invaders decide to destroy all life on Earth. The aliens ___ this ___ plan
                                    by constructing a "space shield" that cuts off all sunlight.

_____ flout _____   9–10. The rule was "No sidewalk vendors on government property," but the
_____ obtrusive _____   vendors seem to have made a conspiracy° to ___ it. They have set up
                                    their tables and stands in a spot that local officials consider ___—right
                                    in front of City Hall.

➤ *Final Check:* Harriet Tubman

Here is a final opportunity for you to strengthen your knowledge of the ten words. First read the following selection carefully. Then fill in each blank with a word from the box at the top of the previous page. (Context clues will help you figure out which word goes in which blank.) Use each word once.

In 1849 Harriet Tubman—then in her late twenties—fled from the (1)_____ heinous _____ brutality she had endured as a slave. Aware that a lone black woman would be a(n) (2)_____ obtrusive _____ figure among ordinary travelers, she traveled on foot and only at night, over hundreds of miles, to reach Pennsylvania. There, for the first time in her life, she was free, but her parents, brothers, and sisters remained behind in Maryland, still slaves. Harriet decided to go back for them—and, over the next ten years, for many more.

Harriet had several qualities that (3)_____ complement _____(e)d each other and facilitated° her mission. First, because she was knowledgeable and had good (4)_____ intuition _____, she could always sense when the time for an escape had arrived, and who could and couldn't be trusted. Second, she was (5)_____ fastidious _____ about planning; she always worked out a plan to the last detail before she (6)_____ implement _____(e)d it. Third, she was flexible, capable of taking (7)_____ impromptu _____ action if an unexpected problem arose. Time and again, when a disaster seemed about to happen, she was able to forestall° it. For instance, when she learned that slave-hunters had posted a description of a runaway man, she disguised him as a woman. When the slave-hunters turned up at a railroad station, she fooled them by having the runaways board a southbound train instead of a northbound one. Fourth, she was (8)_____ discreet _____ about her plans. She knew how important it was to be reticent°, since anyone might be a spy. Often, her instructions about where and when to meet were not actually stated, but were (9)_____ inference _____ s in the songs and Bible stories she used, familiar to those waiting to escape. Fifth, she was physically strong, able to endure extended periods of deprivation°; she could go for a long time without food, shelter, or rest.

Harriet Tubman (10)_____ flout _____(e)d the unjust laws of an evil system, but she was never captured, and she never lost a single runaway. She led more slaves to freedom than any other individual—over three hundred—and her name is venerated° to this day.

Scores	Sentence Check 2 _____%	Final Check _____%	

Enter your scores above and in the vocabulary performance chart on the inside back cover of the book.

CHAPTER

18

auspicious	rebuke
expedite	redeem
extenuating	subordinate
fraudulent	transgress
innuendo	vehement

Ten Words in Context

In the space provided, write the letter of the meaning closest to that of each **boldfaced** word. Use the context of the sentences to help you figure out each word's meaning.

1 **auspicious**
(ô-spĭsh′əs)
-adjective

- The beginning of the semester was **auspicious** for Liza; she got an A on the first quiz and saw this as a promise of more good grades to come.
- Jen and Robert's marriage did not get off to an **auspicious** start. They couldn't agree on what kind of ceremony they wanted or which guests to invite.

c Auspicious means   a. deceptive.   b. indirect.   c. favorable.

2 **expedite**
(ĕks′pə-dīt′)
-verb

- Express lanes in supermarkets **expedite** the checkout process for shoppers who buy only a few items.
- To **expedite** payment on an insurance claim, be sure to include all the necessary information on the form before mailing it in.

a Expedite means   a. to hasten.   b. to reduce the cost of.   c. to delay.

3 **extenuating**
(ĕk-stĕn′yōo-ā′tĭng)
-adjective

- I know I promised to come to the party, but there were **extenuating** circumstances: my car broke down.
- When my father had a heart attack, I missed a final exam. Due to the **extenuating** circumstances, the professor agreed to let me take a makeup exam.

a Extenuating means   a. providing a good excuse.   b. assigning blame.   c. encouraging.

4 **fraudulent**
(frô′jə-lənt)
-adjective

- Leroy was jailed for filing **fraudulent** income tax returns. He had been cheating the government for years.
- The art dealer was involved in a **fraudulent** scheme to pass off worthless forgeries as valuable old paintings.

b Fraudulent means   a. inferior.   b. deceitful.   c. careless.

5 **innuendo**
(ĭn′yōo-ĕn′dō)
-noun

- People weren't willing to say directly that the mayor had taken a bribe, but there were many **innuendos** such as "Someone must have gotten to him."
- When Neil said, "Emily's home sick. Again," he was using an **innuendo**. He really meant that she was just taking another day off.

c Innuendo means   a. a sharp scolding.   b. an obvious lie.   c. a suggestion.

6 **rebuke**
(rĭ-byōok′)
-verb

- When the puppy chews the furniture, don't hit him; instead, **rebuke** him in a harsh voice.
- Although my father scolded me many times in private, I'm grateful that he never **rebuked** me in public.

a Rebuke means   a. to criticize.   b. to make excuses for.   c. to hit.

7 redeem
(rĭ-dēm′)
-verb

- Ricardo's parents were angry with him for neglecting his chores, but he **redeemed** himself by washing and waxing their car.
- Cal was suspended from the basketball team because of his low grades, but he **redeemed** himself the next semester by earning a B average.

<u>b</u> *Redeem* means a. to reveal. b. to make up for past errors. c. to punish.

8 subordinate
(sə-bôr′də-nĭt)
-adjective

- As a waiter, I take orders from the headwaiter, and he's **subordinate** to the manager of the restaurant.
- The federal District Courts are lower than the United States Court of Appeals, which in turn is **subordinate** to the Supreme Court.

<u>a</u> *Subordinate to* means a. lower than. b. a substitute for. c. superior to.

9 transgress
(trăns-grĕs′)
-verb

- Adam **transgressed** by eating an apple Eve gave him; God punished them both.
- Traci knew she had **transgressed** against family wishes when she sold the ring her grandmother had given her.

<u>c</u> *Transgress* means a. to benefit. b. to tell a lie. c. to commit an offense.

10 vehement
(vē-ə′mənt)
-adjective

- I knew my parents would not be happy about my plan to take a year off from school, but I didn't expect their objections to be so **vehement**.
- When Nell's boyfriend slapped her, she responded with **vehement** anger. Yelling "That's the last time you'll ever touch me!" she walked out on him.

<u>a</u> *Vehement* means a. strong. b. secret. c. unjustified.

Matching Words with Definitions

Following are definitions of the ten words. Clearly write or print each word next to its definition. The sentences above and on the previous page will help you decide on the meaning of each word.

1. _____innuendo_____ An indirect remark or gesture, usually suggesting something belittling; an insinuation; a hint
2. _____expedite_____ To speed up or ease the progress of
3. _____rebuke_____ To scold sharply; express blame or disapproval
4. _____vehement_____ Intense; forceful
5. _____fraudulent_____ Characterized by trickery, cheating, or lies
6. _____auspicious_____ Being a good sign; favorable; encouraging
7. _____extenuating_____ Serving to make (a fault, an offense, or guilt) less serious or seem less serious through some excuse
8. _____transgress_____ To sin or commit an offense; break a law or command
9. _____subordinate_____ Under the authority or power of another; inferior or below another in rank, power, or importance
10. _____redeem_____ To restore (oneself) to favor by making up for offensive conduct; make amends

CAUTION: Do not go any further until you are sure the above answers are correct. Then you can use the definitions to help you in the following practices. Your goal is eventually to know the words well enough so that you don't need to check the definitions at all.

➤ *Sentence Check 1*

Using the answer line provided, complete each item below with the correct word from the box. Use each word once.

a. **auspicious**	b. **expedite**	c. **extenuating**	d. **fraudulent**	e. **innuendo**
f. **rebuke**	g. **redeem**	h. **subordinate**	i. **transgress**	j. **vehement**

subordinate 1. The company president is ___ only to the board of directors. She takes orders from the board, and only the board can fire her.

transgress 2. When young children ___, they may lie to cover up their misdeeds.

fraudulent 3. If you get a letter announcing that you've won a free car or free trip in some contest you've never heard of, watch out. It's probably ___.

expedite 4. To ___ the registration process, fill out all the forms before you get in line.

redeem 5. After showing up late for the fund-raising dinner and then falling asleep during the speeches, the politician tried to ___ himself with a public apology.

auspicious 6. According to tradition, it's ___ if March "comes in like a lion" with stormy weather, because it will then "go out like a lamb."

vehement 7. Edna was ___ in her opposition to the proposed budget cuts. She let everyone in the department know just how strongly she felt.

rebuke 8. Later, Edna's supervisor ___(e)d her, saying "No one asked for your opinion about the budget, so just get on with your work."

innuendo 9. The friendly weekly poker game grew less friendly when Travis said, "Isn't it amazing that, week after week, Bill always wins?" The ___, of course, was that Bill was cheating.

extenuating 10. "Yes, my client robbed the bank," the lawyer said, "but there were ___ circumstances. She didn't have time to wait in line to make a withdrawal."

NOTE: Now check your answers to these questions by turning to page 130. Going over the answers carefully will help you prepare for the next two practices, for which answers are not given.

➤ *Sentence Check 2*

Using the answer lines provided, complete each item below with **two** words from the box. Use each word once.

transgress
redeem 1–2. Rudy certainly ___(e)d against decorum° when he showed up at his sister's wedding in jeans. Later, he tried to ___ himself by giving the newlyweds an ostentatious° present.

rebuke
fraudulent 3–4. First the judge ___(e)d the defendants for "violating the public trust." Then he fined them thousands of dollars for engaging in ___ advertising.

auspicious
extenuating 5–6. The tour did not get off to a(n) ___ start—the singer missed the first concert. But there was a(n) ___ reason: he had developed bronchitis, and trying to sing would have exacerbated° the infection.

_____ vehement   7–8. The owner of that company is ___ in his insistence that managers

_____ subordinate   implement° a plan to communicate better with workers in ___ positions.

_____ innuendo   9–10. The restaurant critic wrote, "Those customers who are oblivious° to the

_____ expedite   headwaiter's outstretched hand will have an overly long wait to be
seated." Her ___ implied that customers could ___ getting a table only
by slipping the headwaiter some money.

➤ *Final Check:* Tony's Rehabilitation

Here is a final opportunity for you to strengthen your knowledge of the ten words. First read the following selection carefully. Then fill in each blank with a word from the box at the top of the previous page. (Context clues will help you figure out which word goes in which blank.) Use each word once.

When he was 18, Tony was arrested for possessing a small amount of cocaine. Instead of panicking, he was confident. He didn't think of himself as having (1)____transgress____(e)d; the cocaine was just for fun, not some heinous° offense. On the way to the police station, he wasn't worried about being interrogated°. He figured he could claim that there were (2)____extenuating____ circumstances. He'd say he was just holding the stuff for a friend—maybe he'd even insinuate° that the "friend" was making him the victim of some (3)____fraudulent____ scheme—and then he'd be released right away.

But things didn't work out according to Tony's plans. When he told his story to the police captain, the captain's response was hardly (4)____auspicious____: "Tell it to the judge, kid. I've heard it all before." Then, turning to a(n) (5)____subordinate____ officer, the captain said, "Book him." Tony still wasn't distraught°. He just thought, "Well, my father will extricate° me from this mess. First he'll (6)____rebuke____ me, of course, but after he's through yelling at me, he'll pay my bail. And he knows plenty of influential people who can (6)____expedite____ the legal process so my case will be dismissed quickly." So Tony wasn't prepared for his father's (8)____vehement____ anger, or for his parting words: "You got yourself into this. Now you'll take the consequences."

With no bail, Tony had to wait for his hearing in jail. He was terrified, especially by the other inmates. Some of them tried to start fights with him; others used (9)____innuendo____s, such as calling him "the millionaire." His inference° was that they were threatening retribution° for his easy life. He got through his nine-day stay without being attacked, though, and the experience entirely changed his view of himself. He realized that fooling around with drugs is insidious°—his involvement would only get worse unless he turned his life around.

Therefore, at his court hearing, Tony asked to be sent to a drug treatment center, and as a first-time offender, he got his wish. Today, six years later, Tony is still "clean." And he still wonders what would have become of him if he hadn't managed to (10)____redeem____ himself in his family's eyes—and in his own.

Scores Sentence Check 2 _____%	Final Check _____%

Enter your scores above and in the vocabulary performance chart on the inside back cover of the book.

deride	misconstrue
derogatory	paramount
fabricate	quandary
impending	turbulent
macabre	validate

Ten Words in Context

In the space provided, write the letter of the meaning closest to that of each **boldfaced** word. Use the context of the sentences to help you figure out each word's meaning.

1 **deride**
(dĭ-rīd′)
-verb

- One nightclub comedian **derides** members of the audience, poking fun at their looks, clothing, and mannerisms. He says they know it's just part of the act.
- Walter went on a diet after several classmates **derided** him by calling him "Lardo" and "Blimpy."

_b_ *Deride* means
    a. to misunderstand.   b. to mock.   c. to argue with.

2 **derogatory**
(dĭ-rŏg′ə-tôr′ē)
-adjective

- Lorenzo's **derogatory** remark about his boss—he called her an airhead—caused him to get fired.
- Charisse makes **derogatory** comments about Kareem behind his back, saying that he's vain, sloppy, and lazy. But she never says such things to his face.

_a_ *Derogatory* means
    a. uncomplimentary.   b. mistaken.   c. provable.

3 **fabricate**
(făb′rĭ-kāt′)
-verb

- Supermarket tabloids often **fabricate** ridiculous stories, such as "Boy Is Born Wearing Green Sneakers."
- When she handed in her term paper late, Diane **fabricated** a story that her computer had crashed. The truth is that she doesn't even use a computer.

_c_ *Fabricate* means
    a. to avoid.   b. to prove.   c. to invent.

4 **impending**
(ĭm-pĕnd′ĭng)
-adjective

- Gary never studies until an exam is **impending**. If he'd start sooner, he wouldn't have to cram so hard.
- "Because of the company's **impending** move," the office manager said, "I'm not ordering any supplies until next month, when we'll be in the new office."

_a_ *Impending* means
    a. approaching.   b. apparent.   c. important.

5 **macabre**
(mə-kŏb′rə)
-adjective

- Edgar Allan Poe's story "The Fall of the House of Usher" is a **macabre** tale in which someone is buried alive.
- The movie opened with a **macabre** scene: a row of bodies lying in drawers in the city morgue.

_c_ *Macabre* means
    a. confusing.   b. mocking.   c. gruesome.

6 **misconstrue**
(mĭs′kən-strōo′)
-verb

- Conchita would like to date Matt, but when she told him she was busy last weekend, he **misconstrued** her meaning, thinking she wasn't interested in him.
- Many readers **misconstrue** Robert Frost's well-known line "Good fences make good neighbors." They think it's Frost's own opinion, but the line is spoken by an unneighborly character.

_a_ *Misconstrue* means
    a. to misunderstand.   b. to understand.   c. to ignore.

7 **paramount**
(păr′ə-mount′)
-*adjective*

• When you are driving on rain-slick, icy, or winding roads, good traction is of **paramount** importance, so always be sure your tires are in top condition.

• **Paramount** Pictures must have chosen its name to suggest that its movies were superior to all others.

_a_ *Paramount* means   a. supreme.   b. growing.   c. successful.

8 **quandary**
(kwŏn′də-rē)
-*noun*

• Bonita was in a **quandary**—she couldn't decide whether to return to school, take a job she had just been offered, or move to Alaska with her family.

• Aaron is in a **quandary** over financial matters: he is baffled by the problems of making a budget, handling credit, and paying taxes.

_a_ *Quandary* means   a. a state of confusion.   b. a state of anger.   c. a state of confidence.

9 **turbulent**
(tûr′byōō-lənt)
-*adjective*

• The **turbulent** air made the plane rock so wildly that passengers felt as if they were on a roller coaster.

• The Warreners' household tends to be **turbulent**. Whenever Mr. Warrener gets upset, he yells and throws things.

_a_ *Turbulent* means   a. violent.   b. distant.   c. unusual.

10 **validate**
(văl′ə-dāt′)
-*verb*

• Many people believe Columbus sailed west to **validate** the theory that the world is round. But in 1492, the fact that the world is round was already well known.

• There is no real doubt about the dangers of smoking; the claim that smoking is a serious health risk has been **validated** by many studies.

_b_ *Validate* means   a. to misinterpret.   b. to confirm.   c. to invent.

Matching Words with Definitions

Following are definitions of the ten words. Clearly write or print each word next to its definition. The sentences above and on the previous page will help you decide on the meaning of each word.

1.	*turbulent*	Full of wild disorder or wildly irregular motion; violently disturbed
2.	*macabre*	Suggestive of death and decay; frightful; causing horror and disgust
3.	*quandary*	A state of uncertainty or confusion about what to do; predicament
4.	*derogatory*	Expressing a low opinion; belittling
5.	*validate*	To show to be true; prove
6.	*misconstrue*	To misinterpret; misunderstand the meaning or significance of
7.	*deride*	To make fun of; ridicule
8.	*fabricate*	To make up (a story, information) in order to deceive; invent (a lie)
9.	*impending*	About to happen; imminent
10.	*paramount*	Of greatest concern or importance; foremost; chief in rank or authority

CAUTION: Do not go any further until you are sure the above answers are correct. Then you can use the definitions to help you in the following practices. Your goal is eventually to know the words well enough so that you don't need to check the definitions at all.

➤ *Sentence Check 1*

Using the answer line provided, complete each item below with the correct word from the box. Use each word once.

a. **deride**	b. **derogatory**	c. **fabricate**	d. **impending**	e. **macabre**
f. **misconstrue**	g. **paramount**	h. **quandary**	i. **turbulent**	j. **validate**

macabre 1. Mel has a(n) ___ hobby—he visits places where murders were committed.

paramount 2. We had skipped dinner in order to get to the play on time, so throughout the performance, food—not the drama—was ___ in our thoughts.

impending 3. Just before I was fired, I had a sense of ___ disaster; I could tell that something bad was about to happen.

misconstrue 4. Delia ___(e)d Miguel's friendliness as romantic interest. She didn't realize that he already had a girlfriend.

derogatory 5. When my friend said her teacher was "different," I wasn't sure if she meant the description to be complimentary or ___.

fabricate 6. Dwane didn't show up for the final exam because he hadn't studied, but he ___(e)d a story about having a flat tire.

validate 7. In the psychology class, the students had an interesting team assignment. They had to make some statement about human nature and then ___ it by finding supporting evidence.

quandary 8. Ivan is in a ___ over his car. He doesn't know whether to get his old car the major repairs it desperately needs, take out a loan and buy his dream car, or spend the money he has on another used car he doesn't like.

turbulent 9. The sun may seem to be shining calmly and steadily, but in fact, nuclear reactions inside the sun are causing a seething mass of ___ flames.

deride 10. A critic once ___(e)d a book he disliked by saying, "This is not a novel to be tossed aside lightly. It should be thrown with great force."

NOTE: Now check your answers to these questions by turning to page 130. Going over the answers carefully will help you prepare for the next two practices, for which answers are not given.

➤ *Sentence Check 2*

Using the answer lines provided, complete each item below with **two** words from the box. Use each word once.

turbulent
paramount 1–2. Many surfers prefer ___ water to more uniform waves. Their ___ goal is excitement, and they get a feeling of exhilaration° from confronting a dangerous situation.

quandary
macabre 3–4. I was in a ___ over whether to study, practice the piano, or go to a movie with my friend Sal. To complicate things further, Sal wanted to see a(n) ___ horror film, and I dislike anything gruesome.

validate

fabricate

5–6. When the evidence does not ___ their theories, scrupulous° researchers will report this honestly. But less conscientious researchers will flout° scientific ethics and ___ fake "results" to appear to prove their theories.

impending

derogatory

7–8. With the trial ___, the defense lawyer tried to forestall° negative news stories by asking for a "gag" order. The lawyer argued that if ___ stories about his client's character were published, the trial would be a travesty° of justice.

misconstrue

deride

9–10. When Craig called Peggy "the perfect secretary," she was offended. He was complimenting her, but she ___(e)d his comment, thinking he had ___(e)d her by saying she belonged in a subordinate° position.

➤ _Final Check:_ Rumors

Here is a final opportunity for you to strengthen your knowledge of the ten words. First read the following selection carefully. Then fill in each blank with a word from the box at the top of the previous page. (Context clues will help you figure out which word goes in which blank.) Use each word once.

Did you hear that K-Mart sold sweaters with baby snakes inside? The story, of course, was untrue, but it was not easy to squelch°.

How do such rumors get started? Sometimes they are (1)_____ _fabricate_ _____(e)d. In the case of the K-Mart rumor, the story was actually fraudulent°; someone had deliberately made it up to discredit the store. Often, though, a rumor starts with an innocent misinterpretation. For instance, when a magazine article drew an analogy° between a worm farm turning out bait and McDonald's turning out hamburgers, some readers (2)_____ _misconstrue_ _____(e)d this to mean that McDonald's was grinding up worms in its burgers—and the story quickly spread.

Rumors about individuals can start when someone makes a(n) (3)_____ _derogatory_ _____ statement or (4)_____ _deride_ _____s someone else, out of rancor° or jealousy: "Josie got an A because she's dating Professor X," or "Al isn't in class today— he left town because he knew his arrest for being a Peeping Tom was (5)_____ _impending_ _____." Even an innuendo°—something that's merely hinted at—can start a rumor: "Josie and Professor X are really quite discreet°, aren't they?" No story is too gruesome to make the rounds, not even the (6)_____ _macabre_ _____ tale of the girl whose beehive hairdo housed a black-widow spider, which eventually burrowed into her brain and killed her.

Once a rumor gets started, people who hear it are sometimes in a (7)_____ _quandary_ _____. Even if there's no evidence that the rumor is true, they may be afraid to ignore it. And so rumors continue until they are everywhere, spreading fear, damaging reputations, and turning calm situations into (8)_____ _turbulent_ _____ ones. To stop or forestall° rumors, one thing is probably of (9)_____ _paramount_ _____ importance: before accepting any story, be sure the facts (10)_____ _validate_ _____ it.

Scores	Sentence Check 2 _____%	Final Check _____%

Enter your scores above and in the vocabulary performance chart on the inside back cover of the book.

abrasive	emulate
admonish	hierarchy
antithesis	incapacitate
culmination	prognosis
docile	tumult

Ten Words in Context

In the space provided, write the letter of the meaning closest to that of each **boldfaced** word. Use the context of the sentences to help you figure out each word's meaning.

1 **abrasive**
(ə-brā′sĭv)
-*adjective*

- Pumice stone, a naturally **abrasive** substance, can be used for rubbing away rough spots on the feet.
- Roz has an **abrasive** personality—critical and negative. She always seems to rub people the wrong way.

_b_ *Abrasive* means   a. simple.   b. harsh.   c. common.

2 **admonish**
(ăd-mŏn′ĭsh)
-*verb*

- When the guide found the hikers deep in the woods but unhurt, he **admonished** them for straying off the trail.
- Because the little girl had spent her entire allowance on candy, her parents **admonished** her for wasting her money.

_b_ *Admonish* means   a. to lead.   b. to criticize.   c. to irritate.

3 **antithesis**
(ăn-tĭth′ə-sĭs)
-*noun*

- My taste in music is the **antithesis** of my brother's. I like heavy metal, played loud; he likes soft classical music.
- Pauline's free-spirited second husband is the **antithesis** of her first, who was a very timid and cautious man.

_a_ *Antithesis* means   a. the reverse.   b. something superior.   c. an imitation.

4 **culmination**
(kŭl′mə-nā′shən)
-*noun*

- For an actor or actress, receiving an Academy Award is often the **culmination** of many years of effort, progressing from drama school to bit parts to major roles.
- The Super Bowl is the **culmination** of the entire professional football season. All the rivalries, victories, and defeats lead up to this final contest.

_c_ *Culmination* means   a. a series.   b. a cause.   c. a final high point.

5 **docile**
(dŏs′ĭl)
-*adjective*

- After only a month of obedience training, our uncontrollable puppy calmed down, learned to pay attention to us, and became far more **docile**.
- Drugs and even surgery have been used in mental hospitals to make violent patients **docile**, so that they could be managed more easily.

_a_ *Docile* means   a. obedient.   b. strong.   c. curable.

6 **emulate**
(ĕm′yōo-lāt′)
-*verb*

- Jessie has always tried to **emulate** her older sister; she tries hard to do just as well as her sister—if not better—in school, at sports, and in popularity.
- Youngsters often want to **emulate** famous athletes. They train almost as hard as the champions do, with dreams of someday being as skilled as their heroes.

_b_ *Emulate* means   a. to admire.   b. to imitate.   c. to submit to.

7 hierarchy
(hī′ər-âr′kē)
-noun

- The armed forces are a clear example of a strict **hierarchy**. Everyone has a specific rank and must follow the orders of those whose rank is higher.
- Pam soon learned that all requests and suggestions had to be passed up through the levels of the company **hierarchy**. She could communicate directly with her own boss, but not with the boss's boss—let alone the company president.

_a_ *Hierarchy* means   a. a ranked system.   b. a training system.   c. a large system.

8 incapacitate
(ĭn′kə-păs′ə-tāt′)
-verb

- The lecture was canceled because the speaker was **incapacitated** by the flu.
- My mother can't tolerate alcohol. Even half a glass of wine **incapacitates** her; all she can do is giggle for a while and then go to sleep.

_c_ *Incapacitate* means   a. to irritate.   b. to be concerned with.   c. to disable.

9 prognosis
(prŏg-nō′sĭs)
-noun

- Nathan's operation went well. The surgeon's **prognosis** is that Nathan will fully recover.
- Unless strict legislation is passed to reduce acid rain, the **prognosis** for the world's forests will remain poor.

_a_ *Prognosis* means   a. a forecast.   b. an illness.   c. an organization.

10 tumult
(tōō′mŭlt′)
-noun

- Spectators at a hockey match are often wild and noisy, and the **tumult** becomes even greater during a "sudden-death" overtime.
- On New Year's Eve, the **tumult** in Times Square reached such proportions that the crowd could be heard a mile away.

_b_ *Tumult* means   a. damage.   b. uproar.   c. friction.

Matching Words with Definitions

Following are definitions of the ten words. Clearly write or print each word next to its definition. The sentences above and on the previous page will help you decide on the meaning of each word.

1. _____tumult_____ The noisy disorder of a crowd; a commotion

2. _____incapacitate_____ To make unable or unfit, especially for normal activities; disable

3. _____docile_____ Tending to give in to the control or power of others without resisting; easy to handle or discipline; willingly led

4. _____abrasive_____ Able to cause a wearing away by rubbing or scraping; rough; irritating

5. _____prognosis_____ A prediction of the course, outcome, or fate of something, especially a disease or injury

6. _____admonish_____ To scold gently but seriously

7. _____antithesis_____ The exact opposite

8. _____culmination_____ The highest point or degree or a series of actions or events; the climax

9. _____emulate_____ To try to equal or surpass, especially by imitation; imitate

10. _____hierarchy_____ Organization of people in a series of levels, according to importance or authority

CAUTION: Do not go any further until you are sure the above answers are correct. Then you can use the definitions to help you in the following practices. Your goal is eventually to know the words well enough so that you don't need to check the definitions at all.

➤ *Sentence Check 1*

Using the answer line provided, complete each item below with the correct word from the box. Use each word once.

a. **abrasive**	b. **admonish**	c. **antithesis**	d. **culmination**	e. **docile**
f. **emulate**	g. **hierarchy**	h. **incapacitate**	i. **prognosis**	j. **tumult**

tumult　　　1. At the rock concert, the audience grew more and more excited and out of control. There was such ___ that no one could hear the music.

abrasive　　　2. I ruined a nonstick frying pan by using a(n) ___ cleanser on it—the surface rubbed right off.

incapacitate　　　3. The runner was ___(e)d by a sprained ankle and had to miss the big race.

antithesis　　　4. Wendell's ideas about furniture are the ___ of mine. He likes colonial maple, but I like ultramodern tubular steel.

hierarchy　　　5. The ___ of the Roman Catholic Church goes from the parish priest up through bishops, archbishops, and cardinals, to the Pope at the head.

admonish　　　6. Mother ___(e)d us for spending too much money on her birthday gift, but we could see that she was pleased.

prognosis　　　7. The company is financially sick, and unless some changes are made in top management, the ___ is poor—it could go out of business.

docile　　　8. In the prison movie, the convicts acted very ___ while planning a riot. The guards—who weren't too bright—kept congratulating the inmates on being so well-behaved.

culmination　　　9. In colonial America, many people believed in and feared witches. Hysteria over "witch-hunting" reached its ___ in Salem, Massachusetts, where nineteen supposed witches were put to death.

emulate　　　10. "If you want to ___ Elvis Presley, fine," my mother said. "But try to match his energy and warmth onstage—not his self-destructiveness."

NOTE: Now check your answers to these questions by turning to page 130. Going over the answers carefully will help you prepare for the next two practices, for which answers are not given.

➤ *Sentence Check 2*

Using the answer lines provided, complete each item below with **two** words from the box. Use each word once.

antithesis
docile　　　1–2. The rebellious little girl, always demanding that she get her way, was the ___ of her obedient, ___ sister. They were an incongruous° pair of siblings.

prognosis
incapacitate　　　3–4. The ___ for Dale's arthritis is not encouraging. Her doctor didn't equivocate° but told her frankly that in time it may ___ her completely.

_____hierarchy_____   5–6. Beth moved steadily up the company ___ until she was named
_____culmination_____   president. This appointment, the ___ of twenty years of hard work and
                                 dedication, put her at the zenith° of her career.

_____emulate_____   7–8. Cory has many good qualities that I would like to ___. But his ___
_____abrasive_____   manner is a handicap; he estranges° people because he rejects any ideas
                                 that differ from his own.

_____tumult_____   9–10. Gil didn't expect the children's behavior in the car to be impeccable°,
_____admonish_____   but the ___ in the back seat finally reached such a level that he had to
                                  ___ them.

➤ *Final Check:* Firing Our Boss

Here is a final opportunity for you to strengthen your knowledge of the ten words. First read the following selection carefully. Then fill in each blank with a word from the box at the top of the previous page. (Context clues will help you figure out which word goes in which blank.) Use each word once.

My stint° in the bookkeeping department had lasted for three years when Jay Keller was brought in as department head. I don't expect supervisors to be pals with their subordinates°, and I don't object to being (1)_____admonish_____(e)d when I've done something wrong. Keller's criticism, however, was constant and harsh, and the office atmosphere seemed permeated° by his disapproval of us. His (2)_____abrasive_____ style made everyone in the department miserable. Keller was the complete (3)_____antithesis_____ of Chandra Borden, our previous boss, who had been so thoughtful that we all tried to (4)_____emulate_____ her. In contrast, Keller's mere presence could (5)_____incapacitate_____ us to a point where we could hardly add two and two.

Within a few weeks, even the most (6)_____docile_____ employees were getting rebellious and starting to have subversive° thoughts. Our frustration and anger finally reached a (7)_____culmination_____ when Keller loudly belittled a new worker in front of everyone else, using such derogatory° terms ("Stupid! Airhead!") that he made her cry. Furious, we suddenly decided to go over Keller's head—to ignore the company (8)_____hierarchy_____ and present our complaints about Keller directly to *his* boss.

Our meeting in her office began in (9)_____tumult_____, but then we settled down and told our story, trying to be as lucid° as possible so she could understand exactly what had been going on. We concluded by stating that ours was a deeply troubled department and that if Keller stayed, the (10)_____prognosis_____ for it was not good: everyone else would quit. That was Friday afternoon. On Monday morning, our impromptu° action proved to be successful: we had a new boss.

Scores	Sentence Check 2 _____%	Final Check _____%

Enter your scores above and in the vocabulary performance chart on the inside back cover of the book.

UNIT FOUR: Review

The box at the right lists twenty-five words from Unit Four. Using the clues at the bottom of the page, fill in these words to complete the puzzle that follows.

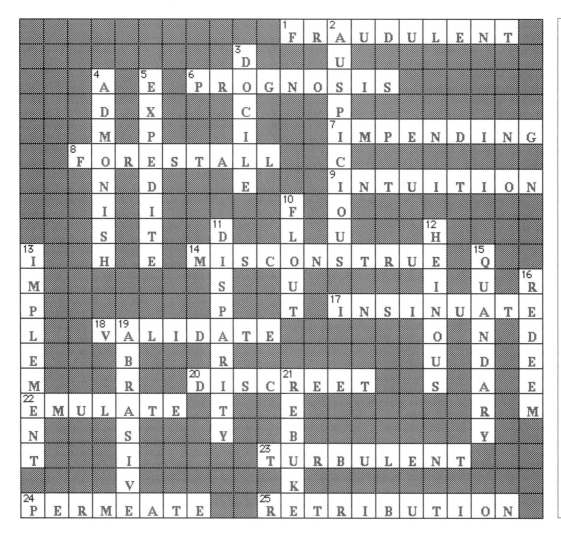

abrasive
admonish
auspicious
discreet
disparity
docile
emulate
expedite
flout
forestall
fraudulent
heinous
impending
implement
insinuate
intuition
misconstrue
permeate
prognosis
quandary
rebuke
redeem
retribution
turbulent
validate

ACROSS

1. Characterized by trickery, cheating, or lies
6. A prediction of the course or outcome of something
7. About to happen; imminent
8. To prevent or hinder by taking action beforehand
9. The ability to know something without reasoning
14. To misinterpret
17. To suggest slyly
18. To show to be true; prove
20. Wise in keeping silent about secrets; prudent; tactful
22. To try to equal or surpass, especially by imitation
23. Full of wild disorder; violently disturbed
24. To flow or spread throughout (something)
25. Something given or done as repayment, reward, or (usually) punishment

DOWN

2. Being a good sign; favorable; encouraging
3. Tending to give in to the control or power of others without resisting; willingly led
4. To scold gently but seriously
5. To speed up or ease the progress of
10. To treat with scorn or contempt
11. An inequality or difference, as in ages or amounts
12. Extremely evil; outrageous
13. To carry out; put into practice
15. A state of uncertainty or confusion about what to do
16. To restore (oneself) to favor by making up for offensive conduct; make amends
19. Able to cause a wearing away by rubbing or scraping; rough; irritating
21. To scold sharply; express blame or disapproval

118

UNIT FOUR: Test 1

Choose the word that best completes each item and write it in the space provided.

incapacitates   1. When my foot falls asleep, it ___ me for several minutes.

    a. interrogates   b. incapacitates   c. validates   d. insinuates

heinous   2. The man's ___ maltreatment of his horses left them crippled and starving.

    a. docile   b. obsequious   c. heinous   d. paramount

subordinate   3. Since my uncle was made vice president of his company, he's ___ only to the president.

    a. subordinate   b. abrasive   c. vehement   d. omnipotent

rebuked   4. The mayor ___ citizens for their lack of cooperation in keeping the parks and streets clean.

    a. emulated   b. rebuked   c. fabricated   d. validated

permeated   5. Harsh rules ___ life in Puritan New England, where people were forbidden even to celebrate Christmas.

    a. emulated   b. permeated   c. derided   d. redeemed

implement   6. For days, Heather planned how she would introduce herself to Ryan, but she never had the courage to ___ her plan.

    a. transgress   b. complement   c. implement   d. admonish

expedite   7. Since I needed the tax forms as soon as possible, I downloaded them from the IRS website to ___ matters.

    a. insinuate   b. forestall   c. expedite   d. deride

omnipotent   8. A novelist once commented on how wonderfully ___ a writer feels when creating "an entire universe."

    a. derogatory   b. omnipotent   c. extenuating   d. insidious

prognosis   9. Since petting an animal appears to lower a person's blood pressure, the ___ for survival after a heart attack is probably better for people with pets.

    a. prognosis   b. culmination   c. innuendo   d. quandary

complement   10. Victor and Diane ___ each other, making a perfect couple. He's rich but doesn't care about money; she's poor and cares about it a lot.

    a. complement   b. fabricate   c. implement   d. validate

(Continues on next page)

PART B

On the answer line, write the letter of the choice that best completes each item.

_a_ 11. You would be most likely to expect a **tumult** in the midst of a(n)
    a. riot.   b. church service.
    c. living room where a family was reading.   d. art museum.

_d_ 12. Although the prisoner appeared at first to be **docile**, prison officials soon learned he was actually
    a. laid-back, relaxed, and cooperative.   b. highly intelligent.
    c. depressed to the point of suicide.   d. rebellious and impossible to discipline.

_a_ 13. People generally use an **innuendo** when they want to say
    a. something critical, but in an indirect way.   b. something highly complimentary.
    c. something that is not true.   d. something in praise of themselves.

_a_ 14. Because Katja felt that her foreign accent was **obtrusive**, she decided to
    a. take a speech class to make it less obvious.   b. keep it because she liked the way it sounded.
    c. assume that no one would notice it.   d. emphasize it.

_c_ 15. Delia knew she must have **transgressed** somehow while driving to work because
    a. she got to work half an hour early.   b. she found herself in a strange neighborhood.
    c. a police car was following her.   d. she got to work half an hour late.

_b_ 16. To **forestall** seeing Diana at school today, Marc
    a. said nasty things to her in the hallway right before classes started.
    b. stayed home.
    c. asked her to eat lunch with him.
    d. ignored her in math class, even though she waved at him.

_c_ 17. One group of students **flouted** the library's "no unnecessary noise" rule by
    a. complaining about other students who were talking loudly.
    b. making occasional, brief whispered comments to one another.
    c. deliberately dropping heavy books on the floor and then laughing.
    d. studying in absolute silence.

_c_ 18. When Peggy came to work late for the third time that week, her boss's **vehement** response was
    a. "Honey, are you having some sort of problem at home?"
    b. "Good morning, Peggy."
    c. "Get out of here and stay out!"
    d. to shake her head and look disappointed.

_b_ 19. Nathan has forgotten his girlfriend's birthday. If he **fabricates** an excuse, he might tell her,
    a. "I forgot. I'm sorry. Can I make it up to you tomorrow?"
    b. "I put the money for your gift in my wallet, and someone stole it."
    c. "Birthdays! Who can remember them? They come along so often!"
    d. "If it will make you feel better, you can forget my birthday next June."

_a_ 20. My brother embarrassed me in front of my date by telling the story of the time I made dinner and the whole family got food poisoning. Later, he **redeemed** himself by
    a. telling another story about me that made me seem brave, funny, and intelligent.
    b. telling even more embarrassing stories about me.
    c. getting into a fight with my date.
    d. asking my date, "Why in the world do you want to go out with her?"

Score   (Number correct) _____ x 4 = _____ %

Enter your score above and in the vocabulary performance chart on the inside back cover of the book.

UNIT FOUR: Test 2

PART A
Complete each item with a word from the box. Use each word once.

a. **abrasive**	b. **antithesis**	c. **emulate**	d. **extenuating**	e. **fraudulent**
f. **hierarchy**	g. **impromptu**	h. **inference**	i. **interrogate**	j. **intuition**
k. **misconstrue**	l. **quandary**	m. **validate**		

abrasive   1. Don't use a(n) ___ cleanser on your car. It will rub the paint off.

inference   2. When Hal refused to kiss his wife goodbye, her ___ was that he was still angry with her.

antithesis   3. Last year, the town experienced a sizzling summer that was the ___ of its frigid winters.

intuition   4. My ___ told me to stay away from anyone who called me "darling" after only five minutes of acquaintance.

emulate   5. I tried to ___ my sister's ability to make money, but I ended up imitating only her readiness to spend it.

interrogate   6. The defending lawyer ___(e)d the witness, asking questions about the witness's relationship to the woman who had been murdered.

fraudulent   7. City streets with names like Oak, Pine, and Elm seem ___ when there aren't any trees on the streets.

quandary   8. Toshiko is in a(n) ___ as to whether she should start college now part-time or wait until she can go full-time.

extenuating   9. The police officer didn't consider my being late for a party a(n) ___ circumstance, so he went ahead and wrote the ticket for speeding.

hierarchy   10. In Andrea's ___ of values, looks are at the top and honesty is at the bottom.

misconstrue   11. "Paris" is the name of a new clothing store, but many people ___ it, thinking it's the name of a French restaurant.

impromptu   12. Acting students often perform ___ scenes. Without a script, they must fully imagine how a particular character might speak and behave.

validate   13. The study ___(e)d claims that drinking is strongly related to violence, providing evidence that alcohol is involved in about half of all murders in the United States.

(Continues on next page)

PART B

Write **C** if the italicized word is used **correctly**. Write **I** if the word is used **incorrectly**.

_C_ 14. Lightning and thunder are signs of an *impending* storm.

_I_ 15. The circus clown's beaming smile and *insidious* makeup made all the children at the party laugh.

_I_ 16. As *obsequious* as ever, Daniel refused to get in line for the fire drill.

_C_ 17. The book's number-one place on the best-seller list was the *culmination* of months of advertising efforts.

_I_ 18. Just as humans often *admonish* each other by shaking hands, elephants often greet each other by intertwining their trunks.

_I_ 19. Bonnie is so *discreet* that the minute someone tells her a secret, she gets on the phone to pass it along.

_C_ 20. It would be fitting *retribution* if my brother, who stays on the phone for hours at a time, had to live in some country with a twenty-year waiting period for phone service.

_C_ 21. Margery's remark about Jeff's new beard was certainly *derogatory*. She said to him, "You look like an armpit."

_I_ 22. We had a *turbulent* day at the park, just relaxing on the grass, snoozing, and enjoying the picnic we had packed.

_C_ 23. There's a large *disparity* in ages between Arlene's two daughters. The elder one is more like a mother to the younger one than a sister.

_I_ 24. Because my friend phoned at an *opportune* time—just before the end of a suspenseful mystery—I hurriedly asked, "Can I call you back?"

_C_ 25. My grandmother was always *fastidious* about her long hair. Now that she's unable to care for herself, we make sure that her hair is as clean and perfectly braided as always.

Score   (Number correct) _____ x 4 = _____ %

Enter your score above and in the vocabulary performance chart on the inside back cover of the book.

UNIT FOUR: Test 3

PART A: Synonyms
In the space provided, write the letter of the choice that is most nearly the **same** in meaning as the **boldfaced** word.

__d__ 1. **redeem**   a) sin   b) leave   c) ask   d) make up for misbehavior

__a__ 2. **insinuate**   a) suggest   b) disagree   c) agree   d) scold

__d__ 3. **prognosis**   a) prevention   b) guess   c) looking back   d) prediction

__b__ 4. **fabricate**   a) admit   b) lie   c) joke   d) err

__b__ 5. **intuition**   a) talent   b) instinct   c) skill   d) memory

__a__ 6. **emulate**   a) imitate   b) admire   c) praise   d) agree with

__d__ 7. **impending**   a) punishing   b) unplanned   c) suggested   d) coming

__c__ 8. **admonish**   a) avoid   b) distract   c) scold   d) dislike

__d__ 9. **opportune**   a) early   b) intense   c) easy to handle   d) well-timed

__d__ 10. **abrasive**   a) unsociable   b) unskilled   c) violent   d) rough

__b__ 11. **extenuating**   a) pleasing   b) excusing   c) delaying   d) creating

__c__ 12. **incapacitate**   a) strengthen   b) discourage   c) disable   d) blame

__d__ 13. **discreet**   a) odd   b) well-planned   c) favorable   d) tactful

__b__ 14. **implement**   a) plan   b) carry out   c) complete   d) delay

__a__ 15. **quandary**   a) dilemma   b) solution   c) sin   d) punishment

__a__ 16. **disparity**   a) inequality   b) tact   c) too little   d) addition

__c__ 17. **validate**   a) question   b) study   c) prove   d) doubt

__b__ 18. **retribution**   a) crime   b) repayment   c) confession   d) innocence

__c__ 19. **implicit**   a) denied   b) questioned   c) suggested   d) omitted

__d__ 20. **vehement**   a) tame   b) wild   c) weak   d) forceful

__b__ 21. **permeate**   a) attack   b) penetrate   c) ease   d) hold off

__a__ 22. **innuendo**   a) indirect remark   b) question   c) opposite   d) impression

__d__ 23. **misconstrue**   a) mistrust   b) misplace   c) mislead   d) misunderstand

__a__ 24. **culmination**   a) high point   b) operation   c) revenge   d) inspiration

__a__ 25. **hierarchy**   a) ranked arrangement   b) imaginary illness   c) forecast   d) end product

(Continues on next page)

PART B: Antonyms
In the space provided, write the letter of the choice that is most nearly the **opposite** in meaning to the **boldfaced** word.

_d_   26. **rebuke**   a) review   b) consider   c) judge   d) praise

_b_   27. **fraudulent**   a) helpful   b) honest   c) friendly   d) hard-working

_a_   28. **omnipotent**   a) powerless   b) unwilling   c) unknown   d) last

_b_   29. **antithesis**   a) opposite   b) same   c) compliment   d) insult

_d_   30. **derogatory**   a) quiet   b) correct   c) smooth   d) flattering

_c_   31. **paramount**   a) weak   b) unsuccessful   c) unimportant   d) unknown

_a_   32. **fastidious**   a) neglectful   b) ignorant   c) far   d) slow

_d_   33. **transgress**   a) change   b) accomplish   c) deny   d) obey

_b_   34. **forestall**   a) prevent   b) encourage   c) enter   d) leave

_c_   35. **complement**   a) substitute   b) imitate   c) clash   d) blame

_d_   36. **docile**   a) clever   b) ungrateful   c) young   d) wild

_d_   37. **subordinate**   a) alike   b) different   c) inferior   d) superior

_a_   38. **auspicious**   a) unfavorable   b) unsatisfied   c) private   d) stated directly

_b_   39. **tumult**   a) loneliness   b) peace and quiet   c) aid   d) slow

_d_   40. **impromptu**   a) implied   b) performed   c) skillful   d) planned

_c_   41. **obsequious**   a) playful   b) tired   c) bossy   d) local

_b_   42. **interrogate**   a) notice   b) answer   c) wonder   d) leave

_c_   43. **heinous**   a) educated   b) talented   c) good   d) reliable

_a_   44. **turbulent**   a) calm   b) interesting   c) faithful   d) clear

_d_   45. **macabre**   a) realistic   b) educational   c) truthful   d) delightful

_b_   46. **flout**   a) catch   b) respect   c) disprove   d) state directly

_a_   47. **obtrusive**   a) inconspicuous   b) polite   c) up-to-date   d) clever

_c_   48. **expedite**   a) remain   b) include   c) delay   d) cover up

_a_   49. **deride**   a) praise   b) suggest   c) explain   d) annoy

_d_   50. **insidious**   a) inconvenient   b) strong   c) expert   d) harmless

Score   (Number correct) _____ x 2 = _____ %

Enter your score above and in the vocabulary performance chart on the inside back cover of the book.

UNIT FOUR: Test 4

Each item below starts with a pair of words in CAPITAL LETTERS. For each item, figure out the relationship between these two words. Then decide which of the choices (*a*, *b*, *c*, or *d*) expresses a similar relationship. Write the letter of your choice on the answer line.

_c_ 1. INSINUATE : HINT ::

    a. hear : see
    c. express : communicate
                      b. exercise : jump rope
                      d. read : calculate

_b_ 2. INTERROGATE : QUESTION ::

    a. hide : see
    c. climb : descend
                      b. investigate : examine
                      d. know : guess

_a_ 3. OMNIPOTENT : HELPLESS ::

    a. sensible : unreasonable
    c. mighty : powerful
                      b. kind : helpful
                      d. recent : new

_c_ 4. OPPORTUNE : WELL-TIMED ::

    a. working : broken
    c. punctual : on time
                      b. delayed : ahead of time
                      d. frequent : rare

_d_ 5. DISCREET : DIPLOMAT ::

    a. hasty : tightrope walker
    c. shy : master of ceremonies
                      b. frail : piano mover
                      d. interesting : speaker

_a_ 6. FASTIDIOUS : NEGLECTFUL ::

    a. cautious : reckless
    c. fatigued : exhausted
                      b. worried : problem
                      d. friendly : neighborly

_c_ 7. HEINOUS : MURDER ::

    a. swift : turtle
    c. destructive : tornado
                      b. minor : catastrophe
                      d. tragic : joke

_b_ 8. AUSPICIOUS : FOUR-LEAF CLOVER ::

    a. threatening : butterfly
    c. time-consuming : toast
                      b. ominous : broken mirror
                      d. disastrous : first prize

_c_ 9. FRAUDULENT : HONEST ::

    a. foolhardy : senseless
    c. stale : fresh
                      b. freakish : odd
                      d. fruitful : productive

_a_ 10. SUBORDINATE : ASSISTANT ::

    a. superior : boss
    c. humorous : librarian
                      b. persistent : architect
                      d. noble : mugger

(Continues on next page)

_b_ 11. DERIDE : PRAISE ::

    a. decide : ignore   b. divide : unite

    c. appear: show up   d. deliver : package

_d_ 12. MACABRE : HORROR FILM ::

    a. old-fashioned : website   b. amusing : math lecture

    c. X-rated : sermon   d. useful : cookbook

_c_ 13. PARAMOUNT : IMPORTANT ::

    a. early : late   b. educational : recess

    c. deadly : unhealthy   d. parallel : intersecting

_c_ 14. TURBULENT : WAR ::

    a. evil : pear   b. few : pounds

    c. tiny : atom   d. desirable : illness

_d_ 15. IMPROMPTU : PREPARED ::

    a. lengthy : boring   b. gown : costume

    c. planned : rehearsed   d. noisy : quiet

_b_ 16. INTUITION : HUNCH ::

    a. instinct : skill   b. logic : deduction

    c. hope : fear   d. invention : copy

_c_ 17. EXPEDITE : DELIVERY ::

    a. extend : deadline   b. delay : departure

    c. accelerate : automobile   d. credit : bill

_c_ 18. ABRASIVE : SCRATCH ::

    a. large : nail   b. pliers : tool

    c. sharp : cut   d. fork : spoon

_d_ 19. INCAPACITATE : BROKEN LEG ::

    a. energize : flu   b. inform : sneeze

    c. entertain : telephone book   d. delay : traffic jam

_b_ 20. HIERARCHY : LEVELS ::

    a. closet : room   b. school : grades

    c. petals : flowers   d. pain : medications

Score   (Number correct) _____ x 5 = _____ %

Enter your score above and in the vocabulary performance chart on the inside back cover of the book.

Appendixes

A. Limited Answer Key

Important Note: Be sure to use this answer key as a learning tool only. You should not turn to this key until you have considered carefully the sentence in which a given word appears.

Used properly, the key will help you to learn words and to prepare for the activities and tests for which answers are not given. For ease of reference, the title of the "Final Check" passage in each chapter appears in parentheses.

Chapter 1 (Apartment Problems)

Sentence Check 1

1. discretion	6. ostentatious
2. detriment	7. vicarious
3. dexterous	8. optimum
4. gregarious	9. sensory
5. scrupulous	10. facetious

Chapter 2 (Hardly a Loser)

Sentence Check 1

1. rudimentary	6. scoff
2. despondent	7. collaborate
3. instigate	8. squelch
4. zealot	9. retrospect
5. venerate	10. resilient

Chapter 3 (Grandfather at the Art Museum)

Sentence Check 1

1. lethargy	6. embellish
2. sporadic	7. juxtapose
3. subsidize	8. dissident
4. inadvertent	9. ambiguous
5. fritter	10. inane

Chapter 4 (My Brother's Mental Illness)

Sentence Check 1

1. regress	6. infallible
2. zenith	7. berate
3. euphoric	8. ubiquitous
4. relinquish	9. maudlin
5. estrange	10. impetuous

Chapter 5 (A Phony Friend)

Sentence Check 1

1. solace	6. sham
2. impeccable	7. propensity
3. predisposed	8. fortuitous
4. solicitous	9. liaison
5. reprehensible	10. equivocate

Chapter 6 (Coco the Gorilla)

Sentence Check 1

1. oblivious	6. cohesive
2. vociferous	7. grievous
3. sanction	8. inundate
4. robust	9. attrition
5. circumvent	10. reticent

Chapter 7 (Our Annual Garage Sale)

Sentence Check 1

1. terse	6. replete
2. indiscriminate	7. relegate
3. bolster	8. nebulous
4. depreciate	9. sedentary
5. tenet	10. inquisitive

Chapter 8 (My Large Family)

Sentence Check 1

1. incongruous	6. exonerate
2. reinstate	7. prolific
3. liability	8. clandestine
4. indigenous	9. superfluous
5. contingency	10. egocentric

Chapter 9 (A Costume Party)

Sentence Check 1

1. travesty
2. notorious
3. provocative
4. grotesque
5. facsimile
6. esoteric
7. mesmerize
8. perfunctory
9. austere
10. Metamorphosis

Chapter 10 (The Missing Painting)

Sentence Check 1

1. contrite
2. plight
3. symmetrical
4. connoisseur
5. verbose
6. conspiracy
7. germane
8. distraught
9. lucid
10. superficially

Chapter 11 (An Ohio Girl in New York)

Sentence Check 1

1. presumptuous
2. adept
3. sordid
4. stint
5. eradicate
6. homogeneous
7. encompass
8. stringent
9. entrepreneur
10. standardize

Chapter 12 (How Neat Is Neat Enough?)

Sentence Check 1

1. repugnant
2. magnanimous
3. masochist
4. foible
5. exhort
6. innocuous
7. rancor
8. recrimination
9. meticulous
10. flamboyant

Chapter 13 (Thomas Dooley)

Sentence Check 1

1. deprivation
2. mitigate
3. exacerbate
4. unprecedented
5. deplore
6. utilitarian
7. objective
8. panacea
9. imperative
10. atrophy

Chapter 14 (Twelve Grown Men in a Bug)

Sentence Check 1

1. decorum
2. tenuous
3. rejuvenate
4. exorbitant
5. exhilaration
6. facilitate
7. extricate
8. espouse
9. synchronize
10. orthodox

Chapter 15 (A Different Kind of Doctor)

Sentence Check 1

1. subversive
2. annihilate
3. staunch
4. criterion
5. proficient
6. holistic
7. emanate
8. analogy
9. vindicate
10. placebo

Chapter 16 (My Devilish Older Sister)

Sentence Check 1

1. permeate
2. forestall
3. opportune
4. interrogate
5. retribution
6. disparity
7. insidious
8. omnipotent
9. insinuate
10. obsequious

Chapter 17 (Harriet Tubman)

Sentence Check 1

1. intuition
2. flout
3. heinous
4. impromptu
5. discreet
6. implement
7. fastidious
8. complement
9. inference
10. obtrusive

Chapter 18 (Tony's Rehabilitation)

Sentence Check 1

1. subordinate
2. transgress
3. fraudulent
4. expedite
5. redeem
6. auspicious
7. vehement
8. rebuke
9. innuendo
10. extenuating

Chapter 19 (Rumors)

Sentence Check 1

1. macabre
2. paramount
3. impending
4. misconstrue
5. derogatory
6. fabricate
7. validate
8. quandary
9. turbulent
10. deride

Chapter 20 (Firing Our Boss)

Sentence Check 1

1. tumult
2. abrasive
3. incapacitate
4. antithesis
5. hierarchy
6. admonish
7. prognosis
8. docile
9. culmination
10. emulate

B. Dictionary Use

It isn't always possible to figure out the meaning of a word from its context, and that's where a dictionary comes in. Following is some basic information to help you use a dictionary.

HOW TO FIND A WORD

A dictionary contains so many words that it can take a while to find the one you're looking for. But if you know how to use guide words, you can find a word rather quickly. *Guide words* are the two words at the top of each dictionary page. The first guide word tells what the first word is on the page. The second guide word tells what the last word is on that page. The other words on a page fall alphabetically between the two guide words. So when you look up a word, find the two guide words that alphabetically surround the word you're looking for.

• Which of the following pair of guide words would be on a page with the word *skirmish*?

   (**skimp / skyscraper**)   **skyward / slave**   **sixty / skimming**

The answer to this question and the questions that follow are given on the next page.

HOW TO USE A DICTIONARY LISTING

A dictionary listing includes many pieces of information. For example, here is a typical listing. Note that it includes much more than just a definition.

> **driz•zle** (drĭz′əl), *v.,* **-zled, -zling,** *n.* — *v.* To rain gently and steadily in fine drops.
> — *n.* A very light rain. —**driz′zly,** *adj.*

Key parts of a dictionary entry are listed and explained below.

Syllables. Dots separate dictionary entry words into syllables. Note that *drizzle* has one dot, which breaks the word into two syllables.

• To practice seeing the syllable breakdown in a dictionary entry, write the number of syllables in each word below.

   gla•mour   _2_   **mic•ro•wave**   _3_   **in•de•scrib•a•ble**   _5_

Pronunciation guide. The information within parentheses after the entry word shows how to pronounce the entry word. This pronunciation guide includes two types of symbols: pronunciation symbols and accent marks.

Pronunciation symbols represent the consonant sounds and vowel sounds in a word. The consonant sounds are probably very familiar to you, but you may find it helpful to review some of the sounds of the vowels—*a, e, i, o,* and *u.* Every dictionary has a key explaining the sounds of its pronunciation symbols, including the long and short sounds of vowels.

   Long vowels have the sound of their own names. For example, the *a* in *pay* and the *o* in *no* both have long vowel sounds. Long vowel sounds are shown by a straight line above the vowel.

   In many dictionaries, the *short vowels* are shown by a curved line above the vowel. Thus the *i* in the first syllable of *drizzle* is a short *i.* The pronunciation chart on the inside front cover of this book indicates that the short *i* has the sound of *i* in *sit.* It also indicates that the short *a* has the sound of *a* in *hat,* that the short *e* has the sound of *e* in *ten,* and so on.

• Which of the words below have a short vowel sound? Which has a long vowel sound?

   drug _short_   **night** _long_   **sand** _short_

Another pronunciation symbol is the *schwa* (ə), which looks like an upside-down *e*. It stands for certain rapidly spoken, unaccented vowel sounds, such as the *a* in *above*, the *e* in *item*, the *i* in *easily*, the *o* in *gallop*, and the *u* in *circus*. More generally, it has an "uh" sound, like the "uh" a speaker makes when hesitating. Here are three words that include the schwa sound:

in•fant (ĭn′fənt)   **bum•ble** (bŭm′bəl)   **de•liv•er** (dĭ-lĭv′ər)

• Which syllable in *drizzle* contains the schwa sound, the first or the second? _____ *second*

Accent marks are small black marks that tell you which syllable to emphasize, or stress, as you say a word. An accent mark follows *driz* in the pronunciation guide for *drizzle,* which tells you to stress the first syllable of *drizzle*. Syllables with no accent mark are not stressed. Some syllables are in between, and they are marked with a lighter accent mark.

• Which syllable has the stronger accent in *sentimental*? _____ *third*

sen•ti•men•tal (sĕn′tə-mĕn′tl)

Parts of speech. After the pronunciation key and before each set of definitions, the entry word's parts of speech are given. The parts of speech are abbreviated as follows:

noun—*n.*   pronoun—*pron.*   adjective—*adj.*   adverb—*adv.*   verb—*v.*

• The listing for *drizzle* shows that it can be two parts of speech. Write them below:

_____ *noun* _____   _____ *verb* _____

Definitions. Words often have more than one meaning. When they do, each meaning is usually numbered in the dictionary. You can tell which definition of a word fits a given sentence by the meaning of the sentence. For example, the word *charge* has several definitions, including these two: **1.** To ask as a price. **2.** To accuse or blame.

• Show with a check which definition (1 or 2) applies in each sentence below:

The store charged me less for the blouse because it was missing a button.   1 _✓_   2 ___

My neighbor has been charged with shoplifting.   1 ___   2 _✓_

Other information. After the definitions in a listing in a hardbound dictionary, you may get information about the *origin* of a word. Such information about origins, also known as *etymology,* is usually given in brackets. And you may sometimes be given one or more synonyms or antonyms for the entry word. *Synonyms* are words that are similar in meaning to the entry word; *antonyms* are words that are opposite in meaning.

WHICH DICTIONARIES TO OWN

You will find it useful to own two recent dictionaries: a small paperback dictionary to carry to class and a hardbound dictionary, which contains more information than a small paperback version. Among the good dictionaries strongly recommended are both the paperback and the hardcover editions of the following:

The American Heritage Dictionary
The Random House College Dictionary
Webster's New World Dictionary

ANSWERS TO THE DICTIONARY QUESTIONS

Guide words: *skimp/skyscraper*
Number of syllables: 2, 3, 5
Vowels: *drug, sand* (short); *night* (long)
Schwa: second syllable of *drizzle*

Accent: stronger accent on third syllable *(men)*
Parts of speech: noun and verb
Definitions: 1; 2

C. Topics for Discussion and Writing

Note: The first three items for each chapter are intended for discussion; the last three, for writing. Feel free, however, to either talk or write about any of the items.

Chapter 1 (Apartment Problems)

1. Athletes training for the Olympics must be **dexterous**. What are some of the other qualities—physical, emotional, and mental—necessary for them to achieve **optimum** results?

2. **Facetious** remarks often communicate serious ideas. An example is this comment by Mark Twain: "One of the most striking differences between a cat and a lie is that a cat has only nine lives." What is the serious meaning behind that remark? What might be the benefit of expressing that meaning in a joking manner?

3. Is it possible to be too **scrupulous** about following rules? Describe a situation in which someone, perhaps an authority figure, was more concerned with the rules than with the welfare of the people involved. Do you agree or disagree with that person's point of view? Explain your answer.

4. Write about a film that gave you an enjoyable **vicarious** experience. Name the film and describe at least one scene that illustrates your point. Begin with a main idea such as this: *The movie _____ gave me a great vicarious experience of being a martial-arts expert.*

5. Did you ever wish you had used more **discretion**? For example, you may have told someone you disapproved of a mutual friend's behavior and later regretted doing so. Write a paper about what you said and why you later regretted saying it. Conclude by telling what you learned from the experience.

6. Who is your most **gregarious** friend or relative? Who is the most shy? In writing, contrast these two people by describing the different ways they react to at least two or three common circumstances, such as being at parties and choosing jobs. Use examples where possible.

Chapter 2 (Hardly a Loser)

1. Do you prefer to work alone on a project, such as a report, or to **collaborate** with others? What are the benefits and drawbacks of each way of working?

2. What are some ways parents and teachers **squelch** children's confidence and creativity? What can they do to encourage children to feel positive about themselves and their abilities?

3. Throughout the ages, **zealots** have **instigated** both good and bad events. What public person or personal acquaintance do you consider a zealot? What do you think makes this person a zealot? Has his or her attitude had good effects—or bad ones?

4. We **venerate** people in a wide variety of fields, from athletics and entertainment to military and religious organizations. Write about a public figure you greatly respect, describing and illustrating the qualities and/or abilities that make you respect this person.

5. Think of a time you behaved in a way that you later regretted. Write about how you acted and how, in **retrospect**, you feel you should have behaved.

6. Has anyone ever **scoffed** at a goal or plan of yours? Write a paper explaining your goal or plan, the other person's comments, and how you reacted. Did you become **despondent** and not follow through? Or were you **resilient** and able to move forward with your idea despite the disapproval?

Chapter 3 (Grandfather at the Art Museum)

1. Some parents and teachers feel that young people **fritter** away their time on video games. Do you agree? Explain what you feel are the good or bad effects of video games on young players.

2. What school activity do you wish a community organization would **subsidize**? Would you like a program giving students internships in various workplaces? A girls' boxing program? Explain and defend the program you name.

3. Tell about a historical, political or religious **dissident** you admire. What did that person oppose? What did he or she achieve? Did the person suffer for his or her views and activities?

4. The ways we **embellish** spaces influence how they make us feel. For instance, a hospital waiting room may be designed to calm and comfort. Write a paper describing the decor of a room with which you're familiar and the effects you think it has.

5. Write about a time you lost out on something (for example, a job) because of **lethargy**—you simply didn't get up enough energy to follow through. **Juxtapose** that story with an account of a time you pursued and achieved something you really wanted. Use this main idea: *Two very different experiences showed me that if I want something, I must take action.*

6. Have you ever made an **inadvertent** comment that was so **inane** you felt embarrassed afterward? Write a paper describing the incident and how you reacted when you realized what you had said.

Chapter 4 (My Brother's Mental Illness)

1. Have you ever **relinquished** a social activity in order to do homework? Or have you ever ignored homework in favor of a social activity? Were you later glad you made the choice you did?

2. Young people may feel **infallible** and behave in **impetuous** and sometimes dangerous ways. What are some examples of such behavior? How might friends help these people avoid harmful, even tragic results?

3. Do you know anyone who has **regressed** to an earlier behavior? For example, you may know someone who began smoking again after having quit. Why do you think this person returned to the old behavior?

4. You have probably seen—or may have been—someone publicly **berated** at school or on the job. Write a paper about such an incident and your reaction to it.

5. Has an argument or a misunderstanding ever **estranged** you from a relative or an old friend? In a paper, explain the situation and what you think can be done, or has been done, to repair the relationship.

6. For many actors, winning an Academy Award is the **zenith** of their career. **Euphoric**, they give emotional speeches thanking others and describing their feelings. Think of an important goal you have achieved. Then write a speech—perhaps one humorously imitating an Academy Award speech—that you could have given upon reaching your goal.

Chapter 5 (A Phony Friend)

1. Some guests on television real-life talk shows become very emotional, even violent. Do you find such behavior **reprehensible**—or acceptable? In your opinion, are these demonstrations genuine, or are they mostly a **sham** and thus not to be taken seriously?

2. Politicians may **equivocate** when answering questions about controversial issues. Why do you think they do this? Can you think of any examples of such deliberate vagueness?

3. When there's a conflict between nations or between a union and a company, a **liaison** is generally called upon to help. Why do you think a go-between is used so often? Why don't the conflicting parties face each other without a mediator?

4. Sometimes when we're sad, a pet can give us **solace** when no one else can. Write a paper on the qualities that enable pets to offer such comfort, using examples you know of.

5. Do you know someone whose appearance or manners seem faultless? Do you consider a certain car or garden to be perfect? Write a paper in which you try to persuade your reader that someone or something is **impeccable**. Include colorful, convincing details in your description.

6. Write about someone who has a **propensity** to get into trouble. Include one or more detailed examples of his or her actions and the trouble that resulted. Also, explain why you think this person is **predisposed** to such situations. Use a main idea such as this: *My brother's habit of acting without thinking often gets him in trouble.*

Chapter 6 (Coco the Gorilla)

1. High-school and college coaches always lose players through **attrition**. What are some ways this happens? How then can a coach create a **cohesive** group of players and mold them into a winning team?

2. Have you ever felt **inundated** with school assignments? Describe study methods you have worked out to help you survive such difficult times. For instance, do you become super-organized? Do you read when you're on a bus?

3. Some students protest in a **vociferous** manner when required to dissect an animal. Do you think these students should be excused from the activity without being punished? Why or why not?

4. When parents divorce, the results can be **grievous** for their children. Some parents explain to their children why they've divorced, while others are **reticent** to do so, feeling they are protecting the children. Write a paper explaining the method you think is more helpful to a child and why.

5. We all want to be **robust**, yet we are sometimes **oblivious** to our own health practices. Think about your own diet and exercise patterns. Then write about two or three ways in which you can improve your chances for remaining healthy and strong.

6. Sometimes, even though we try to **circumvent** an unpleasant situation, we find we have no choice except to become involved. Has this ever happened to you or someone you know? In a paper, describe such a circumstance and what eventually happened.

Chapter 7 (Our Annual Garage Sale)

1. Television news is **replete** with images of violence and disaster. If you were in charge of news programming, would you balance negative news with reports meant to **bolster** viewers' spirits? If so, explain your reasoning and how might you achieve that balance. If not, explain why.

2. Some T-shirts or bumper stickers display **terse** statements that are serious or humorous. What are your favorites? Is there one that particularly expresses a **tenet** by which you live?

3. Do you sometimes go through long periods of being quite **sedentary**? How can people include exercise in their study or work routines?

4. Some people collect items they hope won't **depreciate**, such as stamps. Others collect objects with little financial value, such as matchbooks. Do (or did) you or someone you know collect anything? Write a paper about the collection. How did it start? Which are its most prized items? Is it displayed, or has it been **relegated** to the basement?

5. Write a letter to a friend who has given only **nebulous** thought to a career and could end up making an **indiscriminate** career choice. Explain a way to go about choosing a satisfying occupation. Use some real or imagined examples to make your points clearer and more persuasive.

6. Imagine you are preparing a guide for camp counselors. One section of the guide must tell what to do in rainy weather, when children are stuck inside a room for hours. Write about three or more activities the counselor can lead to occupy the children's **inquisitive** minds and keep them from becoming bored and cranky.

Chapter 8 (My Large Family)

1. On holidays, does your family prepare **superfluous** amounts of food in case uninvited guests show up? Describe how you or relatives overprepare (or underprepare) for such a **contingency**.

2. What are some characteristics and behaviors of **egocentric** people? In what ways might self-centeredness be a **liability** or an advantage?

3. When a defendant in a criminal trial has been **exonerated** of all charges, he or she is set free. What difficulties do you think this person might face in attempting to be **reinstated** into normal life?

4. While Native Americans are **indigenous** to North America, most Americans have roots in other countries. Write a paper on your family's roots and movements from place to place. Trace your family as far back as you can.

5. A friendship between people who appear completely different from each other may seem **incongruous**. Do you know of such a friendship? Write a paper explaining the relationship and the qualities that seem contradictory. Tell what you think draws the friends to each other.

6. Have you ever had to behave in a **clandestine** manner to keep a surprise secret? Write about the surprise and what you had to do to hide it. Here's a sample main idea for this assignment: *Because of a surprise party, I had to become a creative liar.*

Chapter 9 (A Costume Party)

1. At the Academy Awards, some actresses always dress in a **provocative** manner. Why do you think they are so showy in their dress?

2. Mary Shelley's novel *Frankenstein,* the story of a scientist and his **grotesque** creation, has been made into a film several times. Why do you think this story continues to **mesmerize** people?

3. One company makes perfect **facsimiles** of famous paintings, down to the brushstrokes. The copies are sold for much less than the originals. Similarly, laboratory-produced gems are much cheaper than those found in nature. Why do you think people value the originals more than the less expensive copies?

4. Do you study best in a quiet, **austere** environment or a noisy, cluttered space—or something in between? Write a paper on the study setting you prefer. Describe the setting in detail, and tell why you feel it suits you.

5. Some students give only **perfunctory** attention to what happens in class. Write a letter to a teacher telling two or three ways class can be made more interesting for such students.

6. Write the first page or two of a short story, realistic or otherwise, about a **notorious** criminal who tries to undergo a **metamorphosis** in order to escape being recognized and caught by crime fighters.

Chapter 10 (The Missing Painting)

1. Group study can be helpful, but conversations may spring up that aren't **germane** to the study material. Do you prefer to study with friends or by yourself? Or does it depend on the circumstances? Discuss the pros and cons of both study methods, and give reasons for your preferences.

2. Even when people feel **contrite** about something they did, their apology may sound more like an excuse than regret. Think of examples. Why do you think it is difficult for some people to apologize?

3. To avoid being a **verbose** writer, watch for and eliminate unnecessary words. For practice, edit the following statements so that each is only four words: "Hattie was elected to the position of secretary." "At this point in time, I have need of a nap." "I really prefer the dark kind of chocolate." Why might **connoisseurs** of writing recommend this technique?

4. Were you ever so concerned about personal matters that you paid attention only **superficially** to your studies? Were you **distraught** when your limited studying led to low grades? Write about what prevented you from doing well in school and how things turned out.

5. Suppose you have a friend who refuses to recognize a problem with drugs or alcohol. Write a **lucid** letter that might get your friend to admit his or her **plight** and do something to overcome it.

6. Sometimes when nothing seems to go right, we may feel as though there's a **conspiracy** against us. Has this ever happened to you? Write about your experience and how it turned out.

Chapter 11 (An Ohio Girl in New York)

1. Tabloid writers and gossip shows are **adept** at appealing to people's interest in **sordid** events. Why do you think people are so attracted to the information these newspapers and shows offer?

2. Has a **stint** at a part-time or full-time job ever turned into a horrible experience for you? What were the circumstances? Did you quit the job or stick with it?

3. Some schools have a code that **standardizes** student dress. What reasons might they have for this requirement? How do you feel about dress codes, and why?

4. Some teachers have **stringent** standards, while others are easier to satisfy. Write a paper contrasting strict and lenient teachers. Explain, for instance, the differences in their assignments and grading methods. Also tell which type of teacher you prefer and why. You might use the following main idea: *In my experience, a _____ teacher is generally preferable to a _____ one.*

5. Write a paper explaining which habit you would choose to **eradicate** if you could, and why. Go on to name two or three realistic methods you could use to get rid of, or at least weaken, that habit.

6. Imagine you are an **entrepreneur** opening a restaurant chain. Write a description of your business. Include the restaurant's name, theme, decor, and a general description of what the menu would **encompass**.

Chapter 12 (How Neat Is Neat Enough?)

1. When you were a child, did your parents **exhort** you to eat foods you found **repugnant**? What were these foods, and what did you do, if anything, to avoid eating them? How do you feel about these foods today?

2. People's **foibles**, though **innocuous**, can sometimes annoy others. What foibles do your roommates or family members have that sometimes irritate you? Which of your foibles annoy others?

3. Are you **meticulous** about keeping your room and belongings neat, or are you more casual with your environment? Describe what your fellow classmates would see if they were to enter your room right now.

4. Do you know, or know of, someone who is truly **magnanimous**? In a paper, describe that person and tell what he or she has done to deserve your opinion.

5. Sometimes people have an argument that escalates into ongoing **recriminations** and **rancor** that can last for years. Write a paper describing such a conflict and explaining what you think might be done to ease it.

6. Imagine a fictitious person who is very **flamboyant**. Write a paper describing this person's showy appearance and behavior. Also tell what this flamboyance might indicate about his or her nature.

Chapter 13 (Thomas Dooley)

1. When you were a child, did a special treat work as a **panacea** to cure emotional upsets? Is there a certain activity today—listening to music or talking to someone special—that you can count on to lift your blue moods?

2. Being **objective** is **imperative** for a judge and a jury, but it is also important in other areas of life. What are some situations when it's important for people to be objective? For instance, is objectivity important in hiring an employee? In choosing friends?

3. We are surrounded by **utilitarian** things: telephone wires, pencils, television sets, and so on. Name some objects that are *not* utilitarian and are kept solely for aesthetic reasons. Name some utilitarian things we may appreciate for their looks as well as for their usefulness.

4. No matter how much we like television, many of us **deplore** something about it. We may feel that it promotes poor values or that local news shows care more about ratings than news. Write a paper on what you most disapprove of about TV. Include detailed examples.

5. Did someone who tried to help you with a problem actually **exacerbate** the situation? Write about what happened and how you eventually handled your problem.

6. Have you ever worn a cast? How badly did your muscles **atrophy** while in the cast? Was physical therapy used to **mitigate** the muscle weakness? Write a paper about your experience. Tell why you needed to wear the cast and what problems or inconveniences you experienced while wearing it and after removing it.

Chapter 14 (Twelve Grown Men in a Bug)

1. When stressful situations leave you exhausted, do you wish you could get away for a while? If you could take an all-expenses-paid two-week vacation, where would you go and what would you do to **rejuvenate** yourself?

2. Some people feel **exhilaration** when running five miles, whereas others feel it from beating a difficult computer game. What activity fills you with excitement? Explain its appeal to you.

3. What is the worst mess you've ever gotten yourself into? Have you ever made two appointments or dates for the same time and day, or agreed to do something and later wished you hadn't? Describe the situation, and explain how you managed to **extricate** yourself.

4. Have you ever been criticized by someone who **espoused** what you consider an old-fashioned sense of **decorum**? For instance, has a relative insisted that nose piercing is rude or that it's wrong for females to call males for a date? Write a paper about your experience. Describe the situation, the other person's opinion, and your own point of view and reaction.

5. Did you ever want something so much that you paid what seemed like an **exorbitant** price for it? After the purchase, did you still feel it was worth what you paid? Do you or does someone you gave the item to still own it? Write about your experience. Be sure to describe what you bought in a way that shows your reader why you were willing to pay so much for it.

6. Imagine you write an advice column. A fifth grader who has moved to a new school district asks for your ideas on how to **facilitate** his or her adjustment to the new school. For your column, write a letter to that person.

Chapter 15 (A Different Kind of Doctor)

1. Some patients who receive **placebo** remedies report good results, even cures. What do you think could account for these results?

2. Throughout history, the power of persuasion **emanated** from some people so strongly that they were able to influence masses of people. Name some of those people. Did any use their abilities for **subversive** purposes? Explain.

3. In focusing on the whole person, what might a **holistic** physician do that other doctors often do not do? For instance, what life changes might they suggest?

4. Are you a **staunch** fan of a particular sports team? Write a paper explaining what you like about that team. Give examples for all your claims.

5. Were you ever wrongly accused of doing something? If so, were you able to **vindicate** yourself? Write a paper explaining the accusation and its effects upon you. Describe in detail the way you were—or were not—cleared of blame. Feel free to use this main idea: *I learned the hard way how important it is to be careful in making accusations.*

6. Are you good at tennis? An expert baker? Write a paper on an activity in which you feel especially **proficient**. Describe the skill, and tell how you came to acquire it and what place it takes in your life now. Conclude by explaining whether you intend to use the skill in a career or as a hobby.

Chapter 16 (My Devilish Older Sister)

1. Do you so dislike certain activities, such as exercise or doing laundry, that you find ways to **forestall** doing them? Tell which activities you dislike, why you dislike them so much, and what delaying actions you take.

2. Did your parents ever ask you questions like "Where are you going?" and "Who else will be there?" How do young people react to being **interrogated** in this fashion? Are those reactions justified? Why or why not?

3. Do wonderful odors **permeate** your home at certain times of the year, such as particular holidays or seasons? Identify the aromas and the special times with which you associate them.

4. Has anything happened to you at a particularly **opportune** time? For instance, did you get a job offer just when you needed more money? Did you meet someone special right after breaking up with someone else? Write a paper describing one such time in your life, making clear just why the timing of the event was so good. Alternatively, write about an inopportune, or ill-timed, event in your life.

5. Are you good friends with someone despite **disparities** in your opinions, ages, and/or backgrounds? Write about your relationship, explaining the differences between you and how you both handle them so that your friendship is maintained. Has anyone **insinuated** that your friendship is inappropriate? If so, also tell how you dealt with the objection.

6. Have you ever wished to be **omnipotent**? Write a paper describing what you would do and why if you were all-powerful for a day. Include any **retributions** you would like to give out.

Chapter 17 (Harriet Tubman)

1. Imagine you are asked right now to give an **impromptu** speech defending this point: Sports help society. Give one example, fact, or personal experience you could use to support that point.

2. When you get dressed in the morning, are you **fastidious** about choosing accessories to **complement** your outfit? Or are you more casual about your day's attire? Picture this outfit: black shirt, black pants, and black shoes. Name one piece of clothing or jewelry for a male or a female that you feel would complement that outfit.

3. Do you trust your instincts? Tell about a time when you did *not* follow your **intuition** and wished that you had, or a time you *did* follow your instincts and you were, or were not, glad.

4. On New Year's Day, many people decide to begin a self-improvement program. The **inference** is that if they make a New Year's resolution, they will stick with the plan, yet it is often soon forgotten. Have you ever made a resolution (at any time of the year) and actually followed through? Write a paper explaining the resolution and how you **implemented** it. Or write about a resolution you might make in the future and the ways you could carry it out.

5. Have you ever asked a friend or family member to be **discreet** about some information and then discovered it was told to others? Write a paper about your experience and how you handled it.

6. Write the first page or two of a novel about an evil character who **flouts** society's rules. Describe the character and a **heinous** plan he or she is working on.

Chapter 18 (Tony's Rehabilitation)

1. Judges sometimes require people who have **transgressed** but are not violent to **redeem** themselves by doing community work. Do you think community work is a fair punishment? What are the advantages and disadvantages of such a penalty?

2. Some people believe that certain astrological signs are **auspicious** and plan their days accordingly. Do you believe in astrology? Give your opinion and the reasons you feel as you do.

3. What do you do to **expedite** unpleasant chores such as housecleaning or yard work? Explain your methods and why they are helpful to you.

4. Have **extenuating** circumstances ever caused you to miss an important test or appointment? Write a paper a-bout the experience. Describe the circumstances, the reaction to your missing the test or appointment, and what happened in the end.

5. Did you ever harshly **rebuke** someone and later regret it and try to remedy the situation? Write a paper about the experience. Or write about a time you were at the receiving end of **vehement** criticism.

6. What kind of boss would you want to be? Imagine that you are a boss and have asked the workers **subordinate** to you to evaluate your performance anonymously. Write an evaluation you would like to see.

Chapter 19 (Rumors)

1. What do you think are the reasons **macabre** movies are so popular? Give some examples. What do *you* think of such movies, and how do you respond to them?

2. Children sometimes **fabricate** stories, especially when they think they've done something that might get them into trouble. How do you think parents should handle this behavior?

3. Some people are frightened by **turbulent** storms, while others enjoy a lot of lightning and thunder. What is your reaction to violent weather? If you have a pet, how does it react to thunderstorms?

4. Have you ever been in a **quandary** because you wanted to do something your family disapproved of? For example, you might have wanted to buy a car, but your parents wanted you to use the money for college. Write a paper explaining the predicament and the decision you made.

5. Has anyone ever **derided** or criticized something that was of **paramount** importance to you, such as your choice of friends, jobs, or extracurricular activities? Write about the experience, including how you reacted to the ridicule or criticism.

6. Write a paper in which you **validate** one of the following italicized statements with at least two persuasive pieces of evidence—facts, examples, or reasons from your personal experience and common sense. *About everything bad there is something good. School uniforms are a good (or a bad) idea. Music classes benefit students.*

Chapter 20 (Firing Our Boss)

1. Is there someone you would like to **emulate**? The person might be someone you know, a famous individual, or a character in a novel or film. Tell how you'd like to be similar to that person and why.

2. Some people like to work for a large company with a structured **hierarchy**. Others prefer to work for a small business with a more casual structure. Which of these work settings best suits your temperament and career plans? Why?

3. Do you know a couple who are the **antithesis** of one another? For instance, is your uncle very sociable and your aunt shy? Is one person in the couple **abrasive** and the other **docile**? Despite their differences, do the two people seem well suited to each other? Why or why not?

4. Has a politician, athlete, or other public person done something you strongly disapprove of? Write a letter to that person in which you **admonish** him or her and suggest a better behavior.

5. Imagine you are a counselor. Write a professional report about someone who is **incapacitated** by extreme shyness. Describe the person and tell what you think should be done to help him or her. Conclude with what the **prognosis** would be if your program is followed.

6. Graduation day is the **culmination** of years of academic, social, and athletic experiences. Imagine that you are giving a speech at your graduation ceremony. What are some memories you would share with your classmates? What are some words of advice you would give them? Write the speech you would give.

D. Word List

Notes

Notes

Notes

Notes

Notes

Notes